Order My Steps

Other Available Abingdon Press Books
by Marjorie L. Kimbrough

She Is Worthy

Rising with God

MARJORIE L. KIMBROUGH

Order My Steps

Bible Moments to Start the Day

Abingdon Press / Nashville

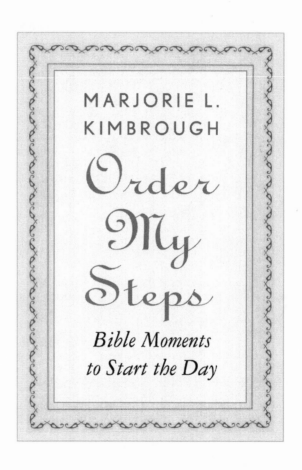

Order My Steps

Bible Moments to Start the Day

This book is printed on acid-free paper.

Library of Congress Cataloging-in-Publication Data has been requested.

ISBN 978-1-4267-5879-9

13 14 15 16 17 18 19 20 21 22—10 9 8 7 6 5 4 3 2 1

MANUFACTURED IN THE UNITED STATES OF AMERICA

For my grandson, Benjamin,

whose steps, I pray, will be ordered by God

Introduction

Well, God, how will you order my steps today? How will you direct my path? How will I know that I am following in your steps and not in my own?

Have you ever wanted to ask those questions? I have, and I seek daily to live in the will of God. I need and want to stay on the path that God has directed for me. I want him to order my steps.

How about you? Do you want God to order your steps? Are you willing to spend time each day seeking his guidance through prayer and meditation? Are you willing to be directed by his will and his word?

Join me as we approach each day seeking spiritual direction.

Order my steps, dear Lord.

In Divine Order

In all your ways acknowledge him,
and he will make straight your paths. Proverbs 3:6

Whenever things work out for the best, my husband says, "It's in divine order." He means that things are working out just as God has planned. God is ordering our steps.

Yet, in order for God to order our steps and make our paths straight, we must acknowledge him. We must seek his direction and give him the praise.

I know someone whose life, according to her orderly birth date, should be in divine order. She was born on January 23, 1945, or 12345. How much more orderly can that be? It is perfect mathematical order. I majored in mathematics in college because I believed that mathematics is most like God. It is perfect, orderly, and can be proven. It is objective. One hundred is perfection; it is no one's subjective opinion.

I want my life to be like that—in divine order. In order for that to happen, God must order my steps; and in order for God to order my steps and make my paths straight, I must acknowledge him. I need to know him. I need to honor him. I need to praise him. I need to worship him. I need to seek his direction in all I say and do.

How about you? Do you want God to order your steps? Do you want him to direct your paths? Are you willing to acknowledge him in all your ways? That's a tall order, but with God's help, it is possible.

Order my steps, dear Lord.

Lord, I need your divine order in my life. Help me to follow your directions every day. Amen.

In what ways have you acknowledged God and felt your paths made straight?

Seeing the Speck

Why do you see the speck in your neighbor's eye, but do not notice the log in your own eye? Matthew 7:3

Can you believe it? Every morning we wake up with a fresh slate full of God's great love and mercies. What a blessing! How will you be renewed and inspired by that great love and compassion today? What will keep your steps ordered by God? Will knowing how much God loves you encourage you to love and show compassion to someone today? Will you think twice about withholding your judgment from a friend or family member? Do you notice the faults of others while you ignore your own?

I met an unwed mother who said as soon as people found out she had children and had never been married, they looked down on her. They wondered how she could have possibly made the same mistake more than once. They ignored the fact she was a loving mother who made many sacrifices for her children and was providing a loving home.

They never considered the possibility that she had learned from her past indiscretions. They did not realize she did not regret having given birth to wonderful children or that she loved them unconditionally. They were not present when the children hugged her and told her how much they loved her. They did not know her children provided her with love and compassion every morning. Isn't it amazing that children are like that? Even if you have to punish them one day, by the next day they are ready to love you all over again. They do not judge you; they don't even notice your shortcomings.

Just today do you think you can extend unconditional love and mercy to those with whom you come in contact? Will you overlook their faults knowing that you have some of your own? Will you follow God's direction?

Order my steps, dear Lord.

Father, thank you for the love and mercy you extend to us in spite of our shortcomings. We don't deserve your grace, but you never tire of extending it to us. Help us to go and do likewise. Amen.

In recent days, what specks have you noticed about your neighbors, and what logs have you ignored about yourself?

A Teachable Spirit

Teach me your way, O LORD,
that I may walk in your truth;
give me an undivided heart to revere your name.
Psalm 86:11

What is it that you really want to learn? Do you want to learn to speak French? Do you want to learn to play an instrument? Do you want to learn more about the Bible and the way God wants to order your steps? What is it that you are committed to learning? *Committed* is the key word. You may want to learn something, but you have not made a commitment. Wanting to learn and committing to learn are two different things.

Before we can make a commitment to learn we must have a teachable spirit. A teachable spirit is an open spirit; it is a willingness to open one's heart and mind and absorb what is presented. Some of us express a willingness to be taught, but we do not have a teachable spirit. We feel that we already know everything. There is no teacher knowledgeable enough to teach us, and there is no information worth learning.

I know that some church members refuse to attend Sunday school or Bible study classes because they feel that they have been church members longer than anyone that might be teaching. They fail to recognize the difference between membership and discipleship. Members join the church; disciples study and prepare to be apostles—those sent to bring others to salvation.

Do you have a teachable spirit? Do you want to be a disciple or are you satisfied with being a member?

Order my steps, dear Lord.

Lord, teach me your way that I may lead others to you.
Amen.

What lessons do you think God has been trying to teach you?

Acceptable Words

Let the words of my mouth and the meditation of my heart
be acceptable to you,
O L*ORD*, *my rock and my redeemer. Psalm 19:14*

What kind of words are acceptable to God? Well, I am sure that they would be kind words. They certainly would not be curse words. They would not be hurtful words, and they would not be discouraging words. Jesus gave us examples of acceptable words in the Sermon on the Mount. He used that teachable moment to tell us what God expects.

Our words ought to be God-controlled. We do not need to speak harsh words to which we have given no thought. Our words ought to be empathetic. We need to feel what the person to whom we are speaking is feeling. We need to speak sincere and honest words that reflect our being pure in heart. We ought to speak words of peace and joy.

Study the verse above a little more closely. Not only do we want our words to be acceptable, but also we want the meditation of our hearts to be acceptable. What does that mean? Before we form the words, we must meditate on them. As we meditate and pray for God's guidance, the words we speak will reflect that guidance and will be acceptable.

How often do we speak without thinking? How often do we try to have the last word and want that word to be a word of revenge or victory? We want to be able to say, "I really told her! I bet she won't say anything else to me." Were those acceptable words? Were they ordered by God?

If God is truly our rock and our redeemer, his strength will sustain us and our words will be acceptable.

Order my steps, dear Lord.

Lord, thank you for leading and guiding me in my meditations and my speech. Amen.

How often do you speak without considering the consequences of your words?

Counting Each Step

Does he not see my ways,
and number all my steps? Job 31:4

Job cries out in frustration because he knows that he has made and has kept a covenant with God. He knows that God sees his ways and numbers his steps. He does not understand why so much calamity has surrounded him. He feels that he is innocent of the sins that might warrant his extreme punishment.

Aren't we like that? We sometimes feel that God has been unfair to us. We look around and see others who have not lived as obediently as we have, yet they have not been punished. Isn't that what is wrong with many of us today? Don't we constantly compare ourselves to others? Why did she get the promotion that I felt I deserved? Why did my child get sick while the children of others escaped the dreaded disease? Why? Why? Isn't God in control? Isn't he counting my steps?

Even after Job's wife and friends try to convince him of his sins and even encourage him to curse God and die, he refuses. He knows that God is still his Redeemer. How about us? No matter what happens are we assured that God is in control? Do we know that God sees us at all times and directs our paths? Are we convinced that God is counting each step and not just some of our steps?

As you move about today, think about Job. Think about the suffering he endured. Is there anything in your life that can compare? Are you ready to accept the fact that you brought nothing into the world and can take nothing out? Do you know that your Redeemer lives? Do you believe that God is counting each step you take?

Order my steps, dear Lord.

Lord, make me aware that you are counting each step I take. I know that if I keep my hand in yours, I will not falter along the path. Amen.

Do you feel that God sees you and is numbering your steps? Why or why not?

Excuses

Moses said to the L*ORD*, *"O my Lord, I have never been eloquent, neither in the past nor even now that you have spoken to your servant; but I am slow of speech and slow of tongue."* Exodus 4:10

How many times have you made an excuse for something you either did not want or know how to do? Rather than simply telling the truth, we make excuses. I contend that an excuse is a half-lie. Some people can come up with fifty-two different excuses for not attending church on Sunday. They really have no interest in attending.

What was Moses' situation? Did he really not want to speak to the people, or did he feel that he did not have the skill and charisma? Note that God told him, "I will be with your mouth and teach you what you are to speak" (Exodus 4:12). Did Moses think that God was not able to deliver on his promises? Why did he ask God to send someone else?

I don't know what Moses was thinking, but I do know that we are just like him. We try to back out of those things we really do not want to do. We claim illness, ignorance, and incompetence. We don't trust God to equip us to do what we know he wants us to do. Sometimes we are even too lazy to prepare to do what we know God has called and commissioned us to do. Why do we make so many excuses? Why do we refuse to allow God to order our steps?

Let's take the time to analyze our actions. Let's determine why we make excuses, and let's tell the truth. We will always find a way to do what we really want to do. We obey our heart's desire, but what does God desire? It's time to stop making excuses and start doing the will of God.

Order my steps, dear Lord.

Holy Father, I don't want to be an excuse-maker. I want to do your will. Equip me. Amen.

Have you ever made an excuse to get out of serving God? If so, why?

Returning to the Familiar

[The Israelites] said to Moses, "Was it because there were no graves in Egypt that you have taken us away to die in the wilderness? What have you done to us, bringing us out of Egypt? Is this not the very thing we told you in Egypt, 'Let us alone and let us serve the Egyptians'? For it would have been better for us to serve the Egyptians than to die in the wilderness." Exodus 14:11-12

How like the Israelites we are when it comes to dealing with new places and circumstances. We want to return to the familiar. We long for what we have been accustomed to even if it was not pleasant. Many times I have heard people say that they were willing to remain in a job they hated because they were at least familiar with the snakes in that environment.

When my grandson, Benjamin, was taken from his one-year-old nursery class to the two-year-old class, he went willingly and seemed to be adjusting well. But, about mid-day he and a classmate made a dash for the door and ran back to their old class. I guess, like the Israelites, he decided that he would rather return to the familiar with all its faults. At least he knew that class and that teacher.

We all resist change. We want to continue operating in a way that has become routine. We don't want to have to learn new methods and new ways of operating. Perhaps we are just basically lazy and resist exploring new territory, or perhaps we are afraid to allow God to order our steps.

Although the Israelites did not trust God to help them survive in the wilderness, God provided for them. They did not die. They were no longer slaves. They had food and shelter even in the wilderness. Moses told them, "Do not be afraid, stand firm, and see the deliverance that the LORD will accomplish for you today; for the Egyptians whom you see today you shall never see again. The LORD will fight for you, and you have only to keep still" (Exodus 14:13-14).

Listen to Moses. Today, when you are longing to return to the familiar, remember that God is with you no matter where you go. He will deliver you and fight your battles. Just keep still.

Order my steps, dear Lord.

Lord, help me step out in faith as I face the unfamiliar today. Amen.

In what situations have you wanted to return to the past or the familiar?

Surviving Rejection

If the world hates you, be aware that it hated me before it hated you. John 15:18

As good and wonderful as Jesus was, he was hated. Why is it then that we expect and pray that everyone will love us? How do we get over the fear of rejection? We must strive to become strong in the face of hatred and rejection. We must work to develop our sense of self-esteem. It is just a fact that everyone will not like us. Some people will even refuse to grant our requests just because they do not like us. We will have some enemies, but we can survive.

To reject means to refuse to accept, grant, or consider. Just think what that could do to one's self-esteem. Is someone refusing to accept me as a person? Is someone refusing to grant my request because they have rejected me as a person? Is someone actually refusing to even consider my request? That could be a real problem.

One has to be secure enough to know that today's refusal is not necessarily tomorrow's refusal, and a denial today is not necessarily denial forever. We have to be willing to ask again, try again, knowing that if we fail to ask, there is no chance that our request will be granted. Jesus did not give up because he was rejected and hated by the world. Neither can we.

Let us begin today to believe that we can survive rejection. Are we not children of the Most High God? Of course we are. It is our Father's good pleasure to grant the requests we have worked for and prayed about. Oh, did I strike a nerve? Did we forget to ask God to order our steps? Are we asking for things or for acceptance we have not worked for or prayed about? If we are, perhaps rejection is appropriate.

Order my steps, dear Lord.

Holy Father, I know it is your good pleasure to grant our requests. Help us do what we need to so that you can bless us. Amen.

Have you ever been rejected? How did you feel about it?

A Prepared Place

In my Father's house there are many dwelling places. If it were not so, would I have told you that I go to prepare a place for you? John 14:2

Have you ever been invited to visit relatives or friends and upon arrival discovered they were not prepared for your visit? You may even have thought that it would have been better if you had made reservations at a hotel. You recall how upon arrival at a hotel (after the designated check-in time), you are given a key and escorted to a room that is prepared for you. You don't have to worry about changing the sheets or sharing a room with a relative or even sharing a bathroom. Everything is prepared for you.

Well, Jesus told us that he was going to prepare a place for us. It will be ready when we arrive. We will have our very own dwelling place because our Father has many dwelling places. I like the translations that say that our Father has many mansions. Somehow *mansions* sounds so much more elegant than *dwelling places*, and I love elegance. But I know how God provides, so I am sure that those dwelling places will be elegant.

Now the only question is how we get to those prepared places. We certainly can't earn a place. We don't have to win a lottery, and we don't have to enter the sweepstakes. We know the way to that prepared place. Jesus is the way. Let us concentrate today on getting to know him better. He has prepared our place, and he will come back to get us. We just have to live like we know him.

Will you be ready to take up residence in that place that God has prepared for you? Have you been living according to his guidance and direction? Have you sought to maintain order in your life?

Order my steps, dear Lord.

Father, thank you for Jesus. He is the way to you and to our prepared place. Amen.

How are you preparing to occupy your prepared place?

Answered Prayer

I will do whatever you ask in my name, so that the Father may be glorified in the Son. John 14:13

Lucas was overloaded with responsibilities on his job. It seemed that the fate of his company depended on him. Just when he figured that he could not bear the stress, he found out that he had throat cancer and needed to go to a larger town for treatment.

Even though it meant being hospitalized more than one hundred miles from home, Lucas and his wife knew that he had to be treated. Although the distance was a problem for his wife, she committed to visiting as often as she could. Their pastor invited her to ride with him whenever he was going to visit.

During one of those visits, the pastor noticed the deep depression into which Lucas had slumped. His treatment had caused blindness in one eye, and Lucas just did not know how he would ever work again. He announced to his wife and his pastor that he wanted to die. He felt that his life was no longer worth living. The pastor immediately asked Lucas and his wife to join him in prayer. There was power in that prayer, and the pastor knew that healing had taken place.

After that prayer, Lucas's demeanor changed, and he realized that he could see out of the previously blind eye. Lucas's doctor entered the room to inform Lucas that there was nothing they could do about his eye. There had been a blood clot, and the damage was irreparable. Lucas told the doctor that everything was fine. God had healed his eye.

The doctor left the room in shock; but Lucas, his pastor, and his wife knew that a miracle had taken place.

Have you ever experienced miraculous healing? Do you believe in miracles? Those whose lives are directed by God do.

Order my steps, dear Lord.

Holy Father, thank you for healing us even when medical professionals believe it is impossible. Amen.

Do you pray in the name of Jesus, and is God always glorified in the answer?

Do We Resemble God?

So God created humankind in his image,
in the image of God he created them;
male and female he created them. Genesis 1:27

The family was gathered in the waiting room nervous and excited about the baby expected to make her appearance momentarily. Who would she look like? Would it be her mother, grandmother, aunt, or some distant relative? Perhaps she'd be like her father's side of the family. I suppose it is natural for the mother to be glad when someone declares, "She looks just like her father!"

Who do we resemble? Perhaps when we were younger, we looked like our sisters, brothers, or cousins; but as we have gotten older, we seem to look more like our parents. We find out that we are starting to exercise their values, pick up their mannerisms, and even repeat some of their favorite sayings. I suppose that is because we've been around them so long and observed them so often that who and what they are or were has rubbed off on us.

What if we could grow to resemble our heavenly Father? We were created in his image. Shouldn't we look and act like him? In order to do that we must spend some time with him. We must know his actions, desires, and expectations. He sent his Son to show us how to live a life of love, service, and devotion to others. Do you really want to be like Jesus in your heart? If you do, you will resemble the One who created you, and everyone will be able to identify you with him. It's up to you—with whom do you choose to be identified?

Order my steps, dear Lord.

Lord, I want everyone I meet to know that I am your child.
Help me look and act like you. Amen.

How do you resemble God?

No Strings

Peace I leave with you; my peace I give to you. I do not give to you as the world gives. Do not let your hearts be troubled, and do not let them be afraid. John 14:27

Have you ever received an unexpected gift and wondered what you were going to have to do to pay for it? You may have wondered whether there were strings attached. Sometimes we receive gifts and know there will be favors owed or gifts that must be given in exchange. You may hear someone say, "I got you this. What did you get me?" I have even heard parents say that they have given their child life, and the child owes it to them to take care of them in their old age. Yes, there are often strings attached.

What gifts are given with no strings? Is the gift of love given with no strings? When we really love someone, don't we expect to be loved in return? Don't we feel hurt and heartbroken when we do everything we can for a loved one only to have them turn their backs on us? Did we do what we did because we loved them or did we really expect to be loved in return?

Jesus gave us a gift with no strings. He gave us peace and told us that he does not give as the world gives. We don't have to worry that we will have to pay him back. We don't have to worry what he will ask for in return. If we believe in him, follow in his way, and allow him to order our steps, we will have peace. We don't even have to worry about what will happen to us after death, for he has gone ahead to prepare a place for us. He has given us the gift of eternal life. There is no way we can pay for that because there are no strings.

Order my steps, dear Lord.

Holy Father, thank you for Jesus who gave to us so freely. He showed us how to live and gave us love, peace, and life eternal. Amen.

Do you live in the peace given to you with no strings? Why or why not?

An Unlikely Angel

Mortals ate of the bread of angels;
he sent them food in abundance. Psalm 78:25

Michael was serving as a missionary in Mexico. He and his wife, Martha, started a Bible study class they hoped would eventually become a church. Although at first their ministry was growing, it suddenly began a rapid decline. Some of their faithful attendees moved away, and others just stopped coming.

While they were wondering what God was saying to them about the decline of their ministry, Martha became pregnant. They were thrilled about the baby, but they had no visible means of support. Michael decided that ministry was not for him, and he looked for what he thought of as a secular job. His job search was unsuccessful.

Martha went into premature labor, was placed on bed rest, and given a prescription to prevent a miscarriage. Michael knew their money was limited. They could buy either food or medicine. He decided to try to protect the baby and bought the medicine. He did not know how to tell his wife there was no money for food.

At the moment of his deepest distress, the doorbell rang. His mother-in-law came in bringing several bags of groceries. She had not been in touch with them and had never seemed to approve of the life Michael and Martha were living.

The appearance of his mother-in-law started a chain of events that led to Michael's finding a job and an opportunity to continue his ministry. God had supplied all of his needs, and of all people, his mother-in-law was God's angel!

Order my steps, dear Lord.

Lord, thank you for thoughtful in-laws who are often labeled mean and uncaring. Amen.

Have you ever experienced a time when you were hungry and an angel brought you food?

Doing All Things

I can do all things through him who strengthens me.
Philippians 4:13

When my husband was pastor of Cascade United Methodist Church in Atlanta, Georgia, the services were closed with the words, "We can do all things in Christ who strengthens us." That, of course, is a paraphrase of a modern translation of Philippians 4:13. Actually, one of the musicians found some music to the words, and the congregation joined hands and sang the verse. It was interesting that the congregation not only joined hands with those next to them in the pews, but they also joined hands across the aisles. They presented a picture of solidarity. At the end of the song, they raised their hands as the pastor said, "And so it is."

Do we really believe that we can do all things? The apostle Paul did. He had been through so many hard times. He had been blinded, beaten, jailed, and shipwrecked, so he knew what Christ could and would do. What have we endured? Could we have said with Paul that we could do all things? How deep is our faith? Do we cease to believe that Christ strengthens us when we suffer hardships and persecutions? Do we surrender to our aches and pains?

Every time today you feel that you cannot endure one more hardship just say, "I can do all things through him who strengthens me." Then think of someone who is suffering more than you are, and pray for their strength. Think of someone who is homeless. Think of someone who is starving. Think of someone who has lost a job or a loved one. Think of someone who has just been informed they have cancer or they will have to lose a limb. There are so many hardships and so little faith.

Now that you have diverted your attention away from your problems, say, sing, and believe, "I can do all things through him who strengthens me." And so it is!

Order my steps, dear Lord.

Thank you, God, for Jesus who strengthens us every day.
Amen.

What things does Christ strengthen you to do?

Only God Knows How Long

Lead me in your truth, and teach me,
for you are the God of my salvation;
for you I wait all day long. Psalm 25:5

Seventy-six year-old Doris Anderson was stranded in the Oregon wilderness for two weeks. She and her husband were on a hunting trip when she went looking for water and then never found her way back. She fell into a deep ravine and could not get out. She thought she had broken her hip, but her injury was not that severe.

Although Doris's husband was rescued later on the day he and Doris were separated, there was no sign of Doris. The area where the search for Doris was conducted was mountainous and rugged. Those searching even looked into the ravine, but did not see Doris.

After three days, many in Doris's family lost hope. They knew that the nights were freezing, and Doris only had the clothes on her back. They were not sure whether she had food besides the small amount she carried with her. How long could she survive?

Her brother-in-law had guessed that maybe Doris could last three days but no longer. His wife insisted that Doris could and would survive as long as she had to. Doris's daughter felt that the Lord had her and would keep her safe, but the search was called off after seven days.

Not three, not seven, but fourteen days passed before rescuers found Doris alive at the bottom of the ravine they had passed many times. Only God knew how long Doris could survive.

What about you? How long could you survive before losing all hope of being found? Is your faith strong enough to sustain you? Do you think you would remember that only God knows how long because he is in control?

Order my steps, dear Lord.

Lord, help us realize that you are the only one who knows how long we can survive. Thank you for rescuing us on time. Amen.

Do you consider yourself to be a patient person? Why or why not?

A Place to Flourish

My Father is glorified by this, that you bear much fruit and become my disciples. John 15:8

How wonderful it is to be able to use all of our God-given talents. As others benefit from and experience our talents, they are often encouraged to praise God for the gifts that we have. I have often listened to singers and praised God for the beautiful voices they have been given. Then I think of all of those who may have such gifts and fail to use them. It has often been said that we use our talents or we lose them.

I thought about a woman who had purchased a beautiful house plant. She looked around her house and thought of the perfect place for the plant. After a few days she noticed the plant was dying. She knew she was taking good care of it and was following the directions for watering it. A friend of hers who was known for having a "green thumb" told her that the plant was not getting the proper light in the place where she had placed it. Although the plant looked good there, it was not the proper place for it to flourish.

How many of us are like that plant? Where we find ourselves is not the place where we can flourish. We may be in the wrong school, majoring in the wrong subject, working at the wrong job, or in the wrong place. We are not flourishing. Like the plant, we are dying. We may be doing what we want to do, but not what God wants us to do. We may not be allowing God to order our steps.

God has given all of us gifts. We need to discover and use them. In that way, we glorify God. We cause others to praise him, and we bear the fruit that proves us to be his disciples. Where can you be planted to flourish?

Order my steps, dear Lord.

Holy Father, thank you for my gifts. Help me use and develop them so that others may see me and glorify you. Amen.

How are you bearing fruit?

Stepping Stones or Stumbling Blocks

They stumble because they disobey the word, as they were destined to do. 1 Peter 2:8b

In his first Epistle the apostle Peter writes to Jewish believers who are struggling in the midst of persecution. They are failing to use God's Word as a stepping stone to Christian living. They are disobeying the word and are stumbling along in life. Does that sound familiar? Do we disobey God's Word and find ourselves stumbling along? Do we stop to recall how different our situation would have been if we had simply obeyed God's direction? We must have forgotten to ask God to order our steps.

Sheila was a married woman, and she had been caught in the bedroom with a married man. Both of their spouses were devastated. They each thought that their marriages were solid—even holy. They had promised to be faithful, to keep their marriage vows; but they had yielded to a temptation that seems to grip many. Why is it that so many ministers, politicians, celebrities, and just plain regular people fall victim to adultery?

What if Sheila and her married partner had obeyed God's word and had not committed adultery? Their keeping that commandment could have been a stepping stone to long and faithful marriages instead of a stumbling block to divorce. They both regretted their actions, but they had not obeyed God's word. Perhaps they had not asked for God's direction when they selected their marriage partners. Perhaps they had not thought about the consequences of infidelity. Perhaps they even thought that they could get away with it. How often do we think that we won't stumble when we disobey God's Word?

Order my steps, dear Lord.

Lord, I want to be obedient to your Word. Amen.

Are we all destined to disobey the Word? Do we all stumble?

Lighted by the Word

Thy word is a lamp unto my feet,
and a light unto my path. Psalm 119:105 KJV

Have you ever driven down a county road at night and discovered that there were no street lights? You could hardly see anything. You might have even been afraid that the road was curving and you might end up in a ditch. You depended totally on your car's headlights, but what would you have done if your headlights had gone out? Think about it. Finding yourself trying to navigate in the dark without light is a very scary situation.

But just how many of us live our lives trying to navigate our problems and challenges without the light of God's Word? We need direction, we need guidance, we need to see where the path of life is leading. We need God to order our steps. We don't know where to walk without having the lamp of God's Word at our feet and its light illuminating our path.

I am sure you are asking: what good is studying a Bible we don't understand and just how can the Word of God help guide me in difficult and challenging situations? Well, as we study the Word of God, we learn of the many who have gone before us guided by the Word. Jochebed risked the life of her child, Moses, to save him from the death ordered for all infant Hebrew boys, and he delivered God's commandments to the people. Esther risked her own life to save her people. Deborah followed God's word and led her people into triumphant battle, and there are so many, many more accounts.

Many times in our lives we will need the light of God's Word to manage our situations. We can be assured that just as God delivered Jochebed, Esther, and Deborah, he will deliver us. All we have to do is trust in God's Word. It is the lamp unto our feet and the light unto our paths.

Order my steps, dear Lord.

Father, give me discernment as I study your Word and learn to follow the light it provides to my path. Amen.

How does God's Word light your path?

Running from a Miracle

Of this gospel I have become a servant according to the gift of God's grace that was given me by the working of his power. Ephesians 3:7

G. Allen Boyd did not know the miracle from which he was running when God called him into the ministry. Although he was a painting contractor, he had started speaking at a few churches when God got his full attention. Once, while riding his motorcycle, he was in a head-on collision with a speeding car.

Allen almost died en route to the hospital. He suffered multiple injuries to his legs, back, and ribs. It was thought he would never walk again. He spent two months in the hospital and had to be transported home by ambulance. He was bedridden at home for eight months, needing an ambulance to go to his doctor's appointments. He spent another year in a wheelchair and finally graduated to crutches. Now he walks using a boot and a brace. The fact that he can walk at all is a miracle.

But the miracle from which he ran was his ministry. Once he was on his feet, he was able to start a church, providing the type of support he knew was needed. Church members support a drug and alcohol rehab center, a missionary in Honduras, and a nursing home. They are also especially proud of their motorcycle, youth, and children's ministries. They celebrate a bikers' day each month, and the focus is on supporting its members and responding to the love of God.

I wonder how many of us are running from the miracle of ministry.

Order my steps, dear Lord.

Lord, what ministry am I running from? Help me recognize and respond to your call. Amen.

Do you consider yourself to be a servant of the gospel? Why or why not?

The Lord's Earth

The earth is the L*ORD's and all that is in it. Psalm 24:1a*

We often hear the words *going green.* This usually refers to doing things to protect the environment and to save the earth's resources. We seem to forget we are not the last people to live on the earth and we need to leave something for the generations to come. Why do we think the earth is ours to do with what we will? The earth is the Lord's.

The story is told of an old man who was planting a carob tree. He was asked how long it would be before the tree would bear fruit. The old man said it would be about seventy years. Then the old man was asked if he expected to be living that long. He replied he did not find the world barren and he would not leave it that way. He knew his ancestors had planted for those who would follow them, and he was doing the same thing.

I wonder if that is our attitude today. It must not be, for suddenly we are all encouraged to go green. We have been using up all the resources we have found, and we are not leaving anything for those who will come after us. I think we have forgotten that the earth is the Lord's. It is not ours. We have been selfish in our use of resources. We have been careless in our disposal of waste, and we have been generous in our pollution of our environment. We have exposed ourselves and future generations to air, noise, chemical, and radiation pollution. We have had to beg people to stop smoking, setting fires, and using chemical weapons. We have acted as though the earth is ours to treat any way we please.

The earth is the Lord's. We have forgotten that we are but temporary tenants. Do you think our treatment of his earth is according to his order?

Order my steps, dear Lord.

Father, forgive us for our selfish occupancy of your land.
Amen.

What do you do to protect and preserve God's earth?

Only Through Prayer

When he had entered the house, his disciples asked him privately, "Why could we not cast it out?" He said to them, "This kind can come out only through prayer."
Mark 9:28-29

The disciples were arguing. I suppose they were upset because they were not able to rid the boy of the spirit that had possessed him. They probably had different opinions as to the proper procedure to follow, but the boy's father knew they had failed.

Jesus came upon the scene in the midst of the argument and asked what was going on. When the situation was explained to him, he was disgusted with his disciples. He had expected them to have greater faith after having been with them for what he considered a long time. The boy's father asked Jesus if he was able to cure the boy. Jesus had to remind the father, his disciples, and all who had gathered that all things can be done for the one who believes. The father immediately expressed his belief and even asked for help with any unbelief.

Are we like that father? Do we say that we believe yet realize that we have some unbelief? Do we go as far as he did and ask for help with our unbelief? Jesus made it clear that all things can be done for those who believe. The kind of belief Jesus was talking about is the kind that has no room for doubt. It is not the kind of belief that wonders if God is able. It is not the kind of belief that only thinks God can.

It is the kind of belief that knows God can do all things, and that kind of belief is cultivated through prayer. We must have a faithful, prayerful relationship with God to believe that he can do all things.

The disciples could not cure the boy because they had not prayed. Have we been faithful in prayer? Have we asked God to direct all of our actions?

Order my steps, dear Lord.

Father, help my unbelief. Amen.

In what ways have you experienced the power of prayer?

Saved by the Dog

When the righteous cry for help, the LORD hears, and rescues them from all their troubles. Psalm 34:17

Danielle was out for her morning run. As usual she was accompanied by her dog, Tazz. Somehow she lost her footing and fell down a sixty-foot cliff. Although she was conscious when she landed, she knew she was badly hurt. She could not walk or even get up, so she tried to crawl. Tazz managed to descend the cliff and reach her. He stayed with her as she crawled about a third of a mile. It took five hours for Danielle to crawl that far. And the day was cold, about twenty degrees.

Knowing that it was getting dark and she could not proceed any further, Danielle stopped. Tazz seemed to know something was wrong, but he refused to leave her side. They slept side by side, keeping each other warm. The next day, noticing that Danielle had not moved, Tazz just kept running back and forth, not knowing what to do. He would run to the top of the cliff and then return to Danielle.

Danielle's neighbors were aware that she had never returned from her run, so they called her father. He called the police, and a search was initiated. The police followed the trail Danielle usually ran and spotted the dog. Tazz would not let anyone touch him. He just kept running toward the cliff. The police followed him, and he led them to Danielle.

Danielle's pelvic fractures were life threatening, but Tazz had saved her. I believe that God had ordered Tazz's steps. He knew what to do. What would you have done?

Order my steps, dear Lord.

Holy Father, you created wonderful, life-saving friends for us. Sometimes those friends are our dogs. Thank you. Amen.

Why are some righteous persons not rescued from trouble? Are they not righteous or does God not hear them?

A Church Without Walls

If a brother or sister is naked and lacks daily food, and one of you says to them, "Go in peace; keep warm and eat your fill," and yet you do not supply their bodily needs, what is the good of that? James 2:15-16

On a Saturday night a pastor was informed that a fire had destroyed the home and possessions of one of the families in his congregation. This family had no insurance and needed assistance. The pastor stopped preparing his Sunday sermon and went to visit the family in their temporary shelter with relatives. They were all cramped and uncomfortable, so the pastor started thinking about how the congregation could respond to this family's needs.

When the congregation met the next day, the pastor told everyone the news and asked how they could help. They decided to dispense with the normal worship service and become a church without walls. They would gather food, clothing, and money and take the worship to the family. The pastor gave the congregation one hour to collect what they could for the family. They were to meet at the temporary shelter.

When they arrived at the relatives' house, they had clothes in all sizes, food enough for everyone, and even a trailer that could serve as temporary housing. One church member in the construction business donated lumber to rebuild. It was amazing what they were able to accomplish in an hour once they had decided to become a church without walls.

They had their worship service outside the small house and the trailer. When they sang, "Blest Be the Tie That Binds," it truly had meaning. I wonder why we don't move the church and worship outside its walls more often.

Order my steps, dear Lord.

Father, help us look outside the physical church and take it where it is needed. Amen.

How have you supplied the bodily needs of another?

Who Do You Know?

I want to know Christ and the power of his resurrection.
Philippians 3:10a

Often people looking for jobs at a particular location try to find out who already works there. They then review the list of employees to see if they know any of them or even if anyone else they know knows any of them. There is the belief that who you know is important.

I guess I wonder why who you know is so important. Should not persons seeking employment concern themselves with what they know? How equipped are they to do the job they are seeking? What experience do they have? What can they offer the employer? How can they contribute to the bottom line?

But we want an inside track to so many things—including employment. It is often easier and faster to have someone we know get us in than it is to take the time to present our qualifications and ourselves as the best one to do the job.

What if we had to apply for salvation? If we did, then who we know would be most important. We have been given the steps to salvation. We have to be able to say that we know Jesus on a first name basis. We have to demonstrate that we communicate with him daily, follow his example for living, love humanity, and are willing to sacrifice greatly for others. Our salvation is dependent upon our knowing, loving, and serving Christ. We cannot just know about him. We must know him. In this case it is important who we know.

Order my steps, dear Lord.

Dear Jesus, help me grow in my love and service to you each day. Amen.

How do you seek to know Christ and the power of his resurrection?

The Parachute Failed

God is our refuge and strength,
a very present help in trouble. Psalm 46:1

Michael Holmes was doing what he had expertly done many times before—he was skydiving. He jumped from a plane at fourteen thousand feet. When he reached four thousand feet, he tried to open his parachute. It seemed to open partially, but he knew that something was wrong. Although he could not see it, the parachute had become entangled in his backpack, which also housed his reserve chute.

Michael knew that he was in trouble, but he began to rely on his extensive training and tried to free the main chute so that the reserve could be deployed. During this harrowing experience he was spinning out of control, making a total of eighty-four revolutions. He also knew that he was rapidly approaching impact with the ground.

Just one thousand feet from the ground, Michael decided to cut away his main chute, pull the chute cable, and try to release his reserve parachute. Nothing worked. He was headed for impact. Remembering that he had a camera on his helmet, he tried to think of an appropriate good-bye to his friends and family. All he could think of was, "I'm dead. Bye." He waved to all who might view his descent.

A fellow skydiving instructor, Jonathan, had jumped with Michael. He watched the whole event, realizing Michael was in real trouble and there was nothing he could do. Michael landed with a loud thud traveling seventy miles per hour, and Jonathan landed near him. God had directed Michael to a blackberry bush near a New Zealand lake. He suffered only a collapsed lung and a broken ankle. Michael's parachute failed, but God didn't! God had truly ordered his steps.

Order my steps, dear Lord.

Lord, we know how often man-made devices fail, but we are thankful that you do not. Amen.

When has God been your present help in trouble?

Fond Memories

The memory of the righteous is a blessing. Proverbs 10:7a

Have you ever been feeling down, even depressed, and then you remembered the smile of a loved one? Did you feel your spirits lift at just recalling the memory? It is amazing that God has equipped us with the ability to remember. We can recall a beautiful sunrise or a breathtaking waterfall. We can recall the first sight of a newborn baby (especially a grandchild) or the look of love on the face of a bride. Our memories can be such a blessing.

But what about the memories that do not lift our spirits? What about those we try so hard to forget? Surely those memories are not a blessing—or are they? When bad memories surround us, let us remember how we survived. Let us remember how God directed our steps and brought us through. Let us recall that we are stronger and wiser than we were before the event that disappointed or frightened us. Then let us concentrate on the goodness of God. God has given us so many more blessings than disappointments. God continues to bless us and provide us with opportunities for even more blessings.

Think of the good times you have spent with someone you love. Remember the words of that book that inspired you. Be still and recall the beautiful music on that favorite CD. Exercise your mind. Recall your blessings. You don't even need a tape recorder or a camera. You have the ability within. God has equipped you. You are blessed!

Order my steps, dear Lord.

Help me, Lord, to store in my internal memory all of the goodness of life and to be grateful. Amen.

How has the memory of a righteous person been a blessing to you?

What Is Your Perspective?

Set your minds on things that are above, not on things that are on earth. Colossians 3:2

The family pet had died and was being buried in the backyard. The children were looking out of the window as the burial was taking place. They had tears in their eyes because they loved the pet very much. The grandfather observed the children and called them over to another window. He encouraged them to look out at the beautiful garden that was just beginning to blossom. There were new buds on the rosebush the children had planted.

The children ran outside to get a closer view. They had smiles on their faces, and they were uplifted with the thought of the beauty that was to come. They had a new perspective on life. They were no longer sad. Their grandfather told them that at first they were looking out of the wrong window.

How often is our perspective distorted because we are looking out of the wrong window? We can concentrate on death and loss or we can rejoice in beauty and new life. Often, the way we feel is determined by our perspective. If we are always looking at the evils and the ugliness of the world, we are saddened and lose all hope. If we are looking at the beauty and goodness of the world, we are strengthened and encouraged and even filled with hope. What window are you looking out of? What is your perspective? How is God directing your vision?

Order my steps, dear Lord.

Father, thank you for the beauty that surrounds us. It gives us encouragement and hope for the future. Help us be constant in our praise and thanksgiving for all of your blessings. Amen.

What heavenly things do you think about?

The Face of God

*For truly to see your face is like seeing the face of God—
since you have received me with such favor. Genesis 33:10b*

Jacob cheated his brother Esau out of his birthright. He ran away from home and built a life for himself and his family. He did not know what had happened to his brother, but he was afraid to meet him face to face.

When Jacob learned that he and his brother were to meet, he sent messengers with presents to appease him. The messengers returned with the report that Esau was coming with four hundred men. Jacob's fear was intensified, and he prayed God would deliver him and his family from the hand of his brother. Then he sought solitude. He spent the night wrestling with a man—perhaps an angel or his own inner spirit. The next morning Jacob was changed. His name was no longer Jacob but it was Israel, for he had wrestled with God and had prevailed.

So, it was a changed Jacob who went to meet Esau. He had a new name and a new confidence. He placed his family behind him and moved ahead, bowing before his brother. But Esau ran to meet him with hugs and kisses. Esau was not interested in the gifts that had been presented, for he had his own wealth. However, Jacob felt a need to provide something to ease his conscience, for he knew he had wronged his brother.

For me, the most important thing about this encounter is that when Jacob looked at his brother's face, he saw the face of God. I wonder how many of us would be able to let the love of God shine on our faces if we encountered someone who had wronged us. Are any of us that forgiving? Let us follow Esau's example. No matter how we have suffered at the hands of another, we can forgive. We can be so consumed with the love of God that his face actually covers our own.

Order my steps, dear Lord.

Father, let others see your face shine through mine. Amen.

Have you ever felt like you have seen the face of God in another?

Room Enough

And she gave birth to her firstborn son and wrapped him in bands of cloth, and laid him in a manger, because there was no place for them in the inn. Luke 2:7

It was cold and raining. A small group of people had huddled together under a bus shelter. They were waiting for the bus and hoping that it would come soon. A mother and her child ran to the shelter, hoping to squeeze in. The people who were already under the shelter did not try to move closer together, so there was no room for the mother and her child.

The child complained of being cold and wanting to get under the shelter, but the mother told her that there was no room. The child commented that it must have been like that when Jesus was born: There was no room for them in the inn. When the people under the shelter heard those remarks, they began to squeeze together, making room for the mother and child.

Even though the people under the shelter had made it appear as though there was no room for the mother and child, there actually was room enough. All the people had to do was make the effort to huddle together. There is always room enough. We have to make the effort to provide it.

I wonder how often we are selfish about the space we need. How often do we take up more room than we need? Do we ever make the effort to share what we have or the space we occupy with others? Do you remember when there was little or no homelessness? People without homes lived with friends or relatives. It was considered the responsibility of family to provide for each other or to help each other "get on their feet." We don't do that anymore. We have forgotten that there is always room enough.

Order my steps, dear Lord.

Lord, let there be room in my heart for others. Amen.

How do you cope with the discovery that there is no room for you—in a hotel, church, class, meeting, workplace?

True Confessions

Since, then, we have a great high priest who has passed through the heavens, Jesus, the Son of God, let us hold fast to our confession. Hebrews 4:14

I was recently reading the true confessions of former First Lady Betty Ford. I was interested in her confessions because I had met her husband when he was president of the United States. He was a kind and humble man, and I wondered about his wife. When I read some of the things to which she had confessed, I was in awe of her truthfulness.

She admitted that severe arthritic pain had led to the overuse and addiction to drugs and alcohol. She confessed that she had felt insecure about her appearance and had felt the need for a face-lift. She often felt unable to bear the pressure of being the first lady.

Mrs. Ford was willing to make her true confessions to the whole world. How willing are we to confess our sins and weaknesses? What are our addictions? How is it that we seek to build our confidence? What steps do we take to improve our appearance? Do we ask God to order our steps?

As we ponder these questions, I wonder how often we confess to God. Do we remember that Jesus is a high priest who can sympathize with our weaknesses because he was tested? We can approach the throne of grace with boldness and receive both mercy and grace to help in time of need (Hebrews 4:15-16).

I am sure Mrs. Ford made her confessions so she could encourage others. She even said she is just like so many others and if she could conquer her weaknesses, so could others. Perhaps we can follow her example and encourage others also by confessing our sins and testifying to the help we have received from the great high priest.

Order my steps, dear Lord.

Father, thank you for sending the great high priest who has walked where we have walked and who understands our temptations. We know that he stands ready to extend grace and mercy in times of need. Amen.

To whom do you confess?

Starting Over

Not that I have already obtained this or have already reached the goal; but I press on to make it my own, because Christ Jesus has made me his own. Philippians 3:12

How often have we wished we could start over or do something over again? We think of the times we have failed to say, "I'm sorry," or we remember that we did not say, "Thank you." Perhaps those two phrases are the most underused phrases in our vocabulary. It means so much to hear someone express regret or appreciation. When someone uses one of these phrases, we go out of our way to show concern and be of assistance.

Even though we may not think it, it is also simple to say, "I love you." We do not say that nearly enough either. Somehow we are embarrassed or believe our love will be misunderstood or misinterpreted. *Love* is also a verb, and we show it in our actions, as well as in our words.

So, if we want to start over by saying those words or phrases that we have often failed to say, today is a good time to begin. All we have to do is begin to incorporate more acts of love in our dealings with others. If we hurt someone's feelings or fail to show support, we can say, "I'm sorry." If something is done for us we did not expect, or if love and concern are shown for us, we can say, "Thank you."

Since love can be a touchy subject, let's start with our family. Start by telling your parents, spouse, siblings, or children how much you love them. Tell them every day. Show them acts of love. Buy some flowers; make some cookies; attend a sporting, school, or church event in which a family member is participating. Take the time to do it. There may not be another opportunity, and you don't want to have any regrets.

Let's start over. Let's show more love and concern. Let's press on to reach the goal for the prize of the heavenly call of God in Christ Jesus.

Order my steps, dear Lord.

Thank you for not being a "one time only" God. You give us many opportunities to start over. Amen.

When have you had to start over to reach your goal?

When Storms Rise

[Jesus] woke up and rebuked the wind, and said to the sea, "Peace! Be still!" Then the wind ceased, and there was a dead calm. Mark 4:39

I can just imagine how the disciples felt when the storm arose. They were afraid. Their boat was being tossed about, and the water was entering places that had been dry. But, most important of all, Jesus was asleep! Did he not care what was happening to them? The disciples woke Jesus up and asked him if he cared.

How many times have we wanted to wake Jesus up and ask him if he really cares what is happening in our lives? It may seem as though we are in that boat with the disciples. Places that had been safe and dry have suddenly become unsafe and wet. Surely Jesus must have forgotten about us or he is asleep.

We may not realize it, but sometimes we need to go through the storm to reach the place of peace and calm.

And sometimes those very turbulent waves lead us to that better place.

A little boy was playing with his toy boat in a creek near his home. There was a sudden gust of wind that caused his boat to sail out of his reach. He knew that he could not venture out into the creek because his mother had warned him of the depth that could drown him. He called to his older brother for help. His brother came and started tossing stones in the water. The boy thought his brother was making things worse, but before long he realized the stones were creating waves that were moving the boat back in his direction. Soon he was able to reach his toy.

Sometimes we face storms in our lives. Each storm creates waves that move us closer to God and to the peace that only he can give. Jesus is not asleep; he is throwing the stones that are causing the waves that will move us closer to the Father.

Order my steps, dear Lord.

Father, I know that you can calm the storms that I experience. Give me the strength and courage to endure the waves that will lead me to your peace. Amen.

What do you do when storms arise in your life?

Too Busy

Therefore I tell you, do not worry about your life, what you will eat or what you will drink, or about your body, what you will wear. Is not life more than food, and the body more than clothing? Matthew 6:25

How many times have you missed the beauty of a sunrise or sunset because you were worrying about your life? How often have you failed to really listen to what your spouse or child was saying? How much money does it take for you to feel financially secure? Just how busy are you? Perhaps you are too busy to notice the important things of life.

A young woman had spent the morning at home. She was bombarded with phone calls. There were so many things she was worried about. She had not noticed the beautiful flowers that were blooming in her yard, and she had not heard her child pleading with her to read a story.

She quickly gathered her belongings and rushed off to a meeting. She did not take the time to talk with her babysitter or to even ask her how she was. She just rushed out, not even taking the time to hug and kiss her child. Just how busy was she? How worried was she about the business of the meeting?

Then, on the way to her meeting, she noticed a traffic sign. Surely she had seen the sign many times before, but this time it seemed to speak to her. The sign said, "Stop, Look, and Listen." She had stopped because a train was coming, but she had not looked around. When she did, she really saw the beauty surrounding her. How had she missed it? She remembered her daughter's pleading to hear a story, and she was ashamed she had not really listened to her. Why was she so rushed and worried? She needed to stop, look, and listen.

The prophet Isaiah wrote, "In returning and rest you shall be saved; / in quietness and in trust shall be your strength" (Isaiah 30:15b). Let us listen to him.

Order my steps, dear Lord.

Lord, teach us to stop, look, and listen. We need to hear from you. Amen.

Are you more likely to worry about money, food, clothing, or health? Why?

Don't You See?

Truly I tell you, many prophets and righteous people longed to see what you see, but did not see it, and to hear what you hear, but did not hear it. Matthew 13:17

Have you ever been looking at something out of the window and called someone to look at it with you? Have you then been disappointed because they did not see what you saw? Did you say, "Don't you see it?" Did you try to give directions by saying, "Look a little to your right or left"?

We often are disappointed because others do not see what we see or understand or interpret things in the same way we do. I think of the way children will insist they see monsters when we are certain there are no monsters around. I have even tried to position myself at their eye level to try to see what they see. There may just be a shadow, which from their perspective looked like a monster.

What does this say to us? Well, we must take the time and put in the effort to really see what others see. We need to try to think of the situation in which someone else finds himself and try to empathize. How would we feel or respond to the situations around us if we were that person?

Jesus told the disciples that he spoke to the crowds in parables because "seeing they do not perceive, and hearing they do not listen, nor do they understand" (Matthew 13:13). Jesus emphasized that we are blessed because we have the opportunity to see and hear and have the meaning revealed. I wonder if we are taking advantage of that opportunity. Don't you see what Jesus did for us?

Order my steps, dear Lord.

Holy Father, we thank you for the great gift of salvation.
Jesus gave us so much more than his life. Help us to see.
Amen.

Why is it that others often do not see things the way you see them or hear what you hear?

Keeping Yesterday's Tools

Jesus Christ is the same yesterday and today and forever.
Hebrews 13:8

Sometimes it is hard to keep up with all the new gadgets we seem to depend on. I often wonder what we did before we had cell phones, the Internet, or microwave ovens. We are often at a loss when our power goes out or some of those new gadgets fail to work.

When the power went out while I was writing, I did not have an old reliable typewriter to turn to; if I had one, I don't think I would have wanted to use it. If I had typed what I was thinking, I would have had to retype it into the computer so it could be saved and transferred to the file I was creating. It just seemed like too much work.

Then I realized that I could still cook. I have always used a gas stove. Even when the power is out, I can use a match to light the burners on the top of the stove and cook the old-fashioned way. As I started to prepare a meal using the burners on the top of the stove, I thought about how really modern that is. In the old days, I would have had to go outside, find wood, and light a fire in a wood-burning stove. All I had to do was strike a match and turn on the gas. Those who have electric stoves are simply out of luck when the power fails.

Then I heard the phone ring. The only house phone that was working was the old one that was not portable. It was attached to the wall, and I could not walk around with it. But I was glad that I had kept at least one such phone.

There are so many old things that become useless to us in the modern day, but Jesus is the same yesterday, today, and forever. We don't have to worry that he will not be important to us because of modern inventions. He will not be replaced by a newer, fancier model. He is here to stay. We still call on him the way our ancestors did and the way our descendants will. Thanks be to God.

Order my steps, dear Lord.

Dear God, thank you for Jesus who is always the same and constantly available to us. Amen.

How are you the same yesterday, today, and forever? How are you different?

Can I Help?

And the king will answer them, "Truly I tell you, just as you did it to one of the least of these who are members of my family, you did it to me." Matthew 25:40

Whenever a family member dies or moves to another location, a call for help seems to go out to family and friends. I am always amazed by the number of casserole dishes, boxes of chicken, and cans of soft drinks that materialize. There is hardly room to store everything. I believe that some of that food is discarded because the close family members do not feel much like eating anyway.

Well, suppose all those people who brought food had volunteered to help close the home of the person who had died. A daughter faced this task alone after her mother's death. There were so many items that meant nothing to the daughter, but the mother had probably felt that she could not live without them. The daughter started the arduous task alone. She started piling up things in front of the house. As people passed by, they looked through the things and stopped to ask if they could have some of them. The daughter was delighted. The more they took, the less she had to dispense with.

Some of those who stopped to ask for things entered the house and volunteered to help with the packing and cleaning. They did not know the family, but felt compelled to help. I wonder if they helped because they had gotten something out of it. Would they have helped if there was nothing in the pile they wanted?

Jesus said that we must minister to the least of these—those who have nothing and can offer us nothing. Are we willing to do that? Do we ask, "Can I help?"

Order my steps, dear Lord.

Lord, I want to help the least of these. I want to respond to your call to the ministry of service. Amen.

Who do you consider the least of these? What have you done for them?

Knowing the Rules

If you wish to enter into life, keep the commandments.
Matthew 19:17c

When I was a college professor, I always prepared a syllabus for my students. I would give specific rules for the class operation, tests, and the dates assignments would be due. I felt that if the students had sufficient time to complete their work, there would be no excuse for being late in turning in assignments or missing tests.

Even though the students knew the rules from the first class, some of them would show up at my office near the end of the semester asking what they needed to do to get an A. I felt as though they thought I was Jesus and, like the rich young ruler, they were asking me what they had to do to be saved. I always responded, "You knew the rules. If you had followed them, we would not be having this conversation."

You see, the students who came to me in the eleventh hour had not done their assignments on time and had often missed classes and tests. It is hard to get an A under those circumstances. So, like the rich young ruler, they went away sorrowful.

I wonder how many of us think we can disobey the rules and still be saved. We want constant grace and mercy. There were some instances (like a family death or illness) in which I would give the student an extension. But usually those who wanted grace really had no reason to request it.

We have a responsibility as Christians and as members of society to obey the rules. We know what they are. We cannot kill, steal, lie, commit adultery, and dishonor our parents or our neighbors. So much of the evil that happens in society is a result of not keeping one of these commandments. We know the rules. If we keep them, we won't have to ask what we must do to be saved.

Order my steps, dear Lord.

Holy Father, Jesus reminded us of the rules you gave Moses; yet, we still fail to keep them. Help us do better. Amen.

What commandments are the hardest for you to keep?

No Static

For God alone my soul waits in silence;
from him comes my salvation. Psalm 62:1

Sometimes static seems to be all around us. There is static on the telephone, and it is hard to hear what the other person is saying. Then there is static on the television or radio, and we cannot understand what is going on. There is even static in our family lives. Everyone talks at once and wants our attention directed to their individual concerns—so much static. During the times of static, all we want is silence.

We may need to retreat to a place of silence. We need to let the static die down. There is a monastery in Illinois that is committed to silence. The monks there have all taken a vow of silence. Communication is done through colors, chimes, and written words. No one speaks. Visitors may enter the monastery if they obey the rules.

I spent a weekend retreat there. It was one of the most interesting retreats I have ever attended. We heard chimes when it was time to eat, and we could point to the food we wanted as we passed through the cafeteria, but we could not speak. Once we had eaten, we returned to our rooms where there was a bed, a lamp, a Bible, and a chair. We were to spend our time in meditation and in silent communion with God. The hope was God would speak to us and we would be open to hearing his voice.

One thought was that we do too much talking to God and not enough listening. Our prayers are filled with words, not silence. God knows our needs, but we feel compelled to reiterate them. I wonder how many of us include a time for listening in our prayers. Do we fill our prayer time talking, asking, and begging? Do we spend any time in silence?

Let's try today to eliminate some of the static in our lives. Although I don't recommend a whole weekend of silence (I almost went crazy), I do recommend an hour or two of just being still and ignoring the static. It is amazing how the static always reappears. It never really goes away. We have to consciously eliminate it. Be still and know that he is God.

Order my steps, dear Lord.

Lord, my soul waits to hear your voice in silence. Speak to me. Amen.

How do you spend time in silence?

A Craving for Mexican Food

[Peter] turned to the body and said, "Tabitha, get up." Then she opened her eyes, and seeing Peter, she sat up. He gave her his hand and helped her up. Then calling the saints and widows, he showed her to be alive. Acts 9:40b-41

Jill Finley's husband, Ryan, could not wake her up. He called 911 after his attempts at CPR failed, and paramedics were able to shock her heart back to response. She was hospitalized and put on a respirator. Although she was breathing, she was in a deep coma. Ryan stayed by Jill's side and read the Bible to her every day. The doctors told Ryan that the chances of Jill's recovery were very slim.

After two weeks in a comatose state, Ryan and Jill's family made the decision to disconnect the machines that were keeping her alive. They said their good-byes and waited for her to stop breathing, but Jill kept breathing on her own. The doctors told Ryan that sometimes it takes a while before the breathing stops. They even told him she might have a last rally and seem to revive. When Jill became restless and started to mumble, Ryan thought she was experiencing her last rally. It soon became clear she was actually waking up. Ryan asked her some simple questions that she quickly and correctly answered. Then she told him she wanted to get out of the hospital and go to her favorite Mexican restaurant. It was a miraculous recovery.

Jill needed speech and occupational therapy, as well as a pacemaker, but she is alive and has learned to cherish each day. She and her husband also cherish every moment they spend together. They know God saved her from a near-death experience and somehow gave her that craving for Mexican food. What are you craving for?

Order my steps, dear Lord.

Lord, thank you for everyday miracles and for the cravings that wake us up wanting to serve you more. Amen.

What are your first thoughts and actions when you wake up?

Come to the Table

At that time Jesus went through the grainfields on the sabbath; his disciples were hungry, and they began to pluck heads of grain and to eat. Matthew 12:1

Jesus believed in feeding hungry people. When the crowds gathered and there was no food, he fed them with a few loaves and fish. When his disciples were hungry on the sabbath, he allowed them to eat. He was not concerned that the Pharisees reminded him that it was unlawful for the disciples to pluck grain on the sabbath. They were hungry, and he was Lord of the sabbath.

Perhaps the need to feed people has always been popular with Christians. They would prepare more than enough food for their families. They would be prepared for that extra guest who needed a place to eat. They never seemed to run out of food; they could say indefinitely, "Come to the table." Even today Christian cooks do the same.

I remember stories of children who were given the least choice piece of chicken, so that the guest could have the meatier piece. Even though those children did not get the piece they wanted, they did not leave the table hungry.

Have we lost that tradition? Do we still know of people who always leave an extra place at the table for an unexpected guest? Those who set an extra place discover that place is always occupied. The guests know that the Christian hostess has left an invitation to come to the table. Perhaps if we continued to pray for God's direction, we would always provide a place at our table.

Order my steps, dear Lord.

Lord, let me be one who always has an extra place at the table. Someone may need to come. Amen.

How are you prepared to feed hungry people?

A Life-Saving Light

The LORD *is my light and my salvation. Psalm 27:1a*

Doug had spent a hot and humid day working. When he got off that night he decided to go to his friend's house for a late-night swim. He had permission to do so whenever he wanted, so he went to the pool. He knew the area well, and although there were no lights on, he changed into his swimming trunks and climbed up the ladder to the diving board. As he climbed the ladder, he imagined how refreshing the cool water would feel, and he was so glad his friend was generous with the use of his pool.

Just as Doug prepared to dive head first into the pool, he saw a brilliant light. He paused and looked more closely. All the lights around the pool were off, even the house lights were off, so where was this light coming from? He decided he had better climb down and check things out more closely. As he descended the ladder, the light seemed to shine more brilliantly. What was it, and where was it coming from?

Doug knelt down beside the pool and looked in. The light had disappeared, but he noticed something else. There was no water in the pool! His friend had obviously drained the pool for its final summer cleaning. That brilliant light had saved him from serious injury or even death. Doug stopped to thank God for that life-saving light!

Order my steps, dear Lord.

Lord, thank you for the light that shines so brightly to save us even from ourselves. Amen.

What lights do you depend on for guidance and direction?

Signs of His Presence

Fools say in their hearts, "There is no God." Psalm 14:1a

A young woman was reading a book her father had read. She loved to read books after her father had read them because he left marks on the pages. He would underline or highlight certain parts that were meaningful to him. That book became a treasure to the woman because she saw signs of the presence of her father.

I have often read a book after my husband has read it. He not only underlines and highlights, he also writes notes in the margins. I read his notes and try to imagine just what he was thinking when he wrote them. In these books I found signs of his presence.

There are so many signs of God's presence in our lives and in our world. I am in awe of the varieties of shades of green that adorn God's trees. I am thrilled by the beautiful and multicolored flowers in yards and surrounding buildings.

It is amazing to see how glorious nature is and how it demonstrates signs of God's presence.

We can take this a step further. We see signs of God's presence when we see neighbors helping each other and strangers giving support to those in need. We see signs of his presence when we notice children clinging to their parents and experiencing unconditional love. We know that type of love could only have been learned from God.

I wonder what signs of our presence we leave in God's world. Do we do more than underline or highlight books? Do we plant beautiful flowers and leave gardens for others to enjoy? Do we raise our children to be a blessing to others? Do we serve God with the gifts and graces he has given us? Are the signs of our presence in the world also signs of his presence in our lives? Think about it.

Order my steps, dear Lord.

Lord, thank you for the many signs of your presence in the world. Help us leave signs of your presence in our lives. Amen.

How would someone know that you had been present?

Spiritual Nourishment

Day by day, as they spent much time together in the temple, they broke bread at home and ate their food with glad and generous hearts, praising God and having the goodwill of all the people. And day by day the Lord added to their number those who were being saved. Acts 2:46-47

In the early Christian church growing together was as much about eating together as it was about doing good deeds. The church was busy rejoicing over the miraculous works of the apostles and the unselfish acts of the followers who sold their possessions to provide for those in need. Yet, even in the midst of all that was happening, eating together seemed to bind the members to each other.

I guess that is why so many churches have Wednesday night suppers and after-church fellowship hours. There is something about sharing a meal that provides spiritual nourishment. We often don't need to eat at these gatherings; in fact, we could really skip a few meals, but sharing food is a source of joy we don't want to miss.

A friend of mine was visiting her dying aunt. The aunt was suffering from incurable cancer and had lost interest in food. My friend knew how much food had meant to her aunt in the past, so she decided to prepare one of her aunt's favorite dishes. Once the meal was prepared, she told her aunt that they would share the meal and talk about some of the things they had enjoyed doing together.

Once they started to eat, the aunt seemed to perk up. She even ate a few bites as she talked about the wonderful experiences she had had in the past. My friend was not sure how much physical nourishment there was in the food, but she knew there was lots of spiritual nourishment. Her aunt died shortly after that meal, but she died with a smile on her face.

We need physical nourishment to survive, but we need spiritual nourishment to fully live. Breaking bread with those we love provides both physical and spiritual nourishment. The early Christian church knew that because God added to their number those who were being saved.

Order my steps, dear Lord.

Lord, we need physical food, but we need spiritual food as well. Thank you for providing both. Amen.

How does food relate to evangelism?

Strength to Endure

I hereby command you: Be strong and courageous; do not be frightened or dismayed, for the Lord *your God is with you wherever you go. Joshua 1:9*

When Moses died, Joshua became the leader. He was not sure he was as strong as Moses was, but God let him know he was not alone. God promised to be with Joshua just as he had been with Moses. God would be with him wherever he went.

What a wonderful promise! Joshua would never be alone. All he had to do was be strong and courageous. He could not be frightened or doubt God's presence. He had to remain faithful, and he had to keep the people faithful to the law.

Perhaps we become weak and fearful when we realize that we have not been faithful to God's law. Just think of how we became fearful before our parents when we knew we had been disobedient. Or remember how frightened we were when the teacher passed out that test for which we had not studied. Somehow when we know we have done what we were supposed to do, fear and dismay seem to disappear.

Young Jason suffered with leukemia most of his life. He endured numerous injections, transplants, and chemotherapy treatments. He was not afraid of needles and he said many times that he had been born brave because God knew what he was going to have to endure. On the other hand, his little brother yelled and screamed every time he saw a needle.

Just before Jason died, he wrote a will. Being as young as he was, he did not have a lot to leave, but he left his brother his bravery. He hoped his brother would no longer be afraid and he would live his life with courage. Jason knew that God had ordered his steps, and he wanted the same thing for his brother.

I pray that we adopt Jason's spirit and realize that God knows what we will have to endure and has equipped us for it. Just as God was with Moses and Joshua, so will he be with us.

Order my steps, dear Lord.

Lord, you have not given us a spirit of fear. Help us be brave. Amen.

How do you know that God is with you wherever you go?

Divine Intervention

We know that all things work together for good for those who love God, who are called according to his purpose.
Romans 8:28

Marlene was going to Europe. She wanted to ride the many trains of Europe. She knew that would be an exciting adventure, and she prayed she would be safe and would have opportunities to be a blessing to those she would meet on the trains.

In Paris she was overwhelmed by the size of the station. There were many fast trains, and she was not sure what platform she needed to proceed to. She asked a conductor for directions and went to the platform to which she had been directed. When she got there, she noticed that the next train did not leave for quite some time. Marlene checked her tickets, sure that her trains had been scheduled much closer together, so she asked an information officer. She discovered that the platform to which she had been directed was not the one she was scheduled for; it was the platform for a later train.

Because it was too late to make it to the platform of the earlier train, so Marlene sat down and tried to relax. When the train arrived, she boarded and found a seat next to a young woman who seemed to be in pain. Marlene started a conversation with her and discovered that her son had recently been killed in an automobile accident. Marlene understood her pain because her brother had also been killed in an automobile accident.

Marlene then began to minister to the woman. She told her how much the church and knowing the love of Jesus had helped her family survive the tragedy. She discussed the love of God and his love for us in the sacrifice of his Son. Marlene assured her God felt her pain and equipped her to survive it. She tried to convey that God orders the steps of those who yield to his direction.

By the time the train had reached its destination, Marlene had made a new friend and been used by God to be a blessing. Marlene remembered she had prayed to be a blessing to those she would meet, and she knew she had not been given directions to the wrong platform. She had been a partner in divine intervention.

Order my steps, dear Lord.

Lord, help us all be a blessing to those with whom we come in contact each day. Amen.

When have you traveled in the wrong direction only to discover that it must have been the way God wanted you to go?

A Miraculous Catch

[Jesus] said to them, "Follow me, and I will make you fish for people." Matthew 4:19

Have you ever seen a great catch in baseball or football? Well, there was a great catch in the Bronx, New York, but the two men involved in the catch did not catch a ball. They caught a toddler.

Julio and Pedro were passing a building when they saw three-year-old Timothy dangling from a fire escape four stories above ground. The toddler had crawled out of a window when his babysitter was not looking. The babysitter could not reach Timothy, so she just yelled for help. It was up to Julio and Pedro. They positioned themselves beneath the fire escape and prepared as best they could to catch the boy.

Timothy fell, hitting Pedro in the chest so hard that he was knocked off balance, but then he bounced into Julio's arms. It was indeed a miraculous catch.

Timothy was treated at the hospital, but he only had a cut on his forehead. Both Julio and Pedro were uninjured and proud they had saved Timothy from death or serious injury. Timothy's mother, who was working at the time of the accident, was grateful to the men and thankful to God. She said Timothy was smiling and happy after his rescue.

It was a miracle that Julio and Pedro were passing by at the time Timothy fell, and it was a miracle that they were willing and able to catch him. God was directing them.

Order my steps, dear Lord.

Lord, thank you for positioning your servants at the right place at the right time. Amen.

What does it mean to fish for people?

Looking for Direction

Jesus said . . . , "I am the way, and the truth, and the life. No one comes to the Father except through me. If you know me, you will know my Father also. From now on you do know him and have seen him." John 14:6-7

When I travel to an airport with which I am not familiar, I look for signs that will lead me in the direction I want to go. Sometimes the signs are confusing or the arrows posted with them seem to point nowhere, but somehow I usually find the way. Even as I follow these signs, I think of people who either cannot see well or cannot see at all. How do they know the direction in which they want to proceed?

Some airports provide a sighted person to lead the challenged traveler; in other places challenged travelers have to ask another traveler for directions. They may be fortunate enough to encounter someone who is not so pressed for time that he or she will pause and direct them correctly.

We all need directions at some point in our lives. Where do we look? Are we dependent on signs or people?

Jesus answered that question for us. He told us, "I am the way." We need to follow his directions. He told us he could point us to the truth and the life. He could and would point us to the Father. That should be the direction we wish to go.

But what of those who say they cannot see Jesus? It becomes our responsibility to let them see him in us. We have to be that compassionate traveler who takes the time to direct the sightless person. We have to be the Christian who visits the sick and cares for the elderly. We have to be the one to whom young people come for advice and counsel. We have to be the way for them just as Jesus is the way for us.

In what direction are you traveling today? Can you see the signs? Do you see Jesus?

Order my steps, dear Lord.

Lord, I want to point the way to Jesus. Help me. Amen.

How can you point the way to Jesus?

God Never Sleeps

At noon Elijah mocked them, saying, "Cry aloud! Surely he is a god; either he is meditating, or he has wandered away, or he is on a journey, or perhaps he is asleep and must be awakened." 1 Kings 18:27

Elijah challenged the Israelites to make a decision. He told them that they could not continue to go along limping with two different opinions. He said, "If the LORD is God, follow him; but if Baal, then follow him" (1 Kings 18:21b). The people did not respond, so Elijah devised a test to determine the true God. They were to place a prepared bull on wood, and the god who sent fire to the wood would be the true God. The people agreed with this test.

When Baal's prophets called on their god, there was no response. Elijah made fun of them and told them perhaps their god was away or was sleeping. He knew his God never slept. He was always available.

After several hours and futile attempts to get Baal to respond, Elijah took over. He used twelve stones, representing the tribes of the sons of Jacob, to repair the altar that had been torn down. After placing wood and the prepared bull on the altar, he had the people pour water on the altar three times. Then he called on the true God to send fire. The fire consumed the bull, the wood, the stones, and all the water.

Elijah made sure that the people of Israel realized their God never slept. He was always available to them. He deserved their worship and their praise.

I know that sometimes we become discouraged, and we think God is asleep. It seems that God just does not hear us or does not respond as rapidly as we think he should. We may even turn to relatives and friends, but we often discover that they are busy or disinterested or sleeping. God is the only one we can depend on every moment of every day. God never sleeps. Call on him.

Order my steps, dear Lord.

Father, I know you are always available to me. Help me wait patiently for your response. Amen.

What makes you know that God never sleeps?

Tumbleweed

God is our refuge and strength,
a very present help in trouble. Psalm 46:1

In February of 2008, the state of Tennessee was hit with thunderstorms and a tornado. Thirty-two lives were lost, approximately two hundred people were injured, and hundreds of homes were destroyed. On the morning after the storm, emergency workers were looking for survivors. They spotted what they thought was a doll lying face down on the ground about one hundred yards from a house that had been split right down the middle. They knew that a woman and her child had lived in the house, and they had already discovered the woman's body.

As they approached the doll, they discovered that it was not a doll at all, but a baby. The baby was breathing, and they rushed him to the hospital. The baby had a collapsed lung and numerous cuts and scrapes, but he was alive. It was a miraculous discovery!

One of the workers had thought what he saw was tumbleweed, for the baby had been tossed around by the wind. Although it was a lighthearted suggestion, the nickname, "Tumbleweed" stuck.

Tumbleweed is now living with his grandparents who are thrilled they have this miraculous reminder of the daughter they lost in the storm. It seems that he smiles and loves music just the way his mother did. He is a source of hope in the midst of so much destruction.

This miraculous discovery attracted the attention of many well-wishers, and a trust fund was established to pay for Tumbleweed's education. His grandmother said that a baby food company sent a package that included a spoon engraved with the name *Tumbleweed.*

Although he was mistaken for a doll and even for wind-tossed tumbleweed, he was a miraculous discovery. God had provided a path of discovery for him and a plan of happiness for his grandparents.

Order my steps, dear Lord.

Lord, thank you for saving the baby and bringing joy in the midst of sorrow. Amen.

How does God show himself in natural disasters?

Comforted by the Word

O taste and see that the LORD *is good;*
happy are those who take refuge in him. Psalm 34:8

When I was first diagnosed with breast cancer, I was convinced God was using me as an instrument to do ministry with other women. I felt confident I would be completely cured and there would be many opportunities for me to minister to others. I was not wrong. I have been cancer free for fifteen years, and I have helped many others deal with their disease.

The first decision my husband and I made was for me to have a lumpectomy followed by radiation. The cancer was discovered in its early stages, and chemotherapy was not needed. Although that was a blessing, one oncologist thought that every woman with breast cancer should have chemotherapy so they could appreciate the devastation of the disease. He could not understand my upbeat attitude. He told me when the knowledge that I had the disease really registered, I would cry and wail. I never went to his office again, for I knew that God was ordering my steps. There was no need for weeping and wailing.

I approached my six weeks of radiation with the 34th psalm. As soon as I arrived at the radiology clinic, I started reciting the psalm. The verses "I sought the LORD, and he answered me, / and delivered me from all my fears" (verse 4) and "O taste and see that the LORD is good; / happy are those who take refuge in him"(verse 8) were comforting. So, I memorized Psalm 34, and it continues to minister to me. I especially remember the lines that say, "My soul makes its boast in the LORD . . . / O magnify the LORD with me, / and let us exalt his name together" (verses 2a, 3). Just think of boasting in and about the Lord and magnifying his name while going through radiation.

I also like the part of the psalm that says, "Come, O children, listen to me; / I will teach you the fear of the LORD" (verse11). I suppose that verse speaks to me because I taught Sunday school to little children for many years. It was always heartwarming to see the eyes of those children light up when they came to realize the love of God. I remember one little boy who loved Sunday school so much that whenever he saw me at church, he would say, "Let's have Sunday school." I would try to explain that it was not Sunday, but he would just look at me and say, "I have my money." Of course, he figured that we were both at church and he had his offering, so having Sunday school was a definite possibility.

The psalm ends with the words "The LORD redeems the life of his servants; / none of those who take refuge in him will be condemned" (verse 22). Repeating those words assures me of the blessings we have at all times, and we, in turn, ought to bless the Lord at all times.

Order my steps, dear Lord.

Your praise, O Lord, is continually on my lips. I will bless you at all times. Amen.

How have you taken refuge in God when making a health decision?

A Gift of Love

For God so loved the world that he gave his only Son, so that everyone who believes in him may not perish but may have eternal life. John 3:16

Tye Johnson's fiancée, Jarena Bates, needed a miracle. She was suffering from kidney failure. The only thing that could save her from numerous dialysis treatments was a kidney transplant.

Jarena's best prospect for a compatible kidney was a family member. Both her mother and sister went to the hospital to be tested, but medical conditions prevented Jarena's mother from being a donor, and her sister was not a match. Tye had driven them to the hospital and volunteered to be tested in her mother's place. Although it was a long shot, he matched. Tye knew it was a miracle and he had an opportunity to give a gift of love to the woman he loved. He remembered that God loved the world so much that he gave his Son, and Tye loved Jarena enough to give her his kidney. Tye felt that giving his kidney would be following God's directions.

Jarena was not sure Tye should donate a kidney because there could be complications for him, but he said that he was committed to her through sickness and health and the transplant would bring them closer together. She would literally have a part of him.

The transplant was successful. Tye suffered no ill effects, and Jarena's prognosis is excellent. It was a gift of love. God had brought them together both physically and spiritually.

Order my steps, dear Lord.

Father, we thank you for the miraculous gift of Jesus. Help us adopt that loving spirit of giving. Amen.

Is there anyone for whom you would give your life?

A Miraculous Operation

Have faith in God. Truly I tell you, if you say to this mountain, "Be taken up and thrown into the sea," and if you do not doubt in your heart, but believe that what you say will come to pass, it will be done for you.
Mark 11:22b-23

Brooke Zepp was diagnosed with a rare and fatal inoperable tumor. The tumor was malignant, entangled in arteries, and buried deep in her abdomen. Just trying to remove the tumor would damage the organs whose blood supply came from the arteries in which it was entangled. Brooke knew it was hopeless, and she decided to prepare for death by getting her affairs in order.

But transplant surgeon Dr. Tomoaki Kato believed he could perform a miraculous operation. His idea was to perform a two-step procedure. First, he would remove all of the affected organs from her body. Second, he would remove the tumor. He knew it would be ground-breaking surgery, and it would take at least fifteen hours. Brooke knew that she had nothing to lose and everything to gain, so she agreed to the surgery. It certainly seemed better to take a chance on living rather than submitting to an early death. Brooke believed that the idea for the surgery had come from God.

Dr. Kato removed Brooke's stomach, pancreas, spleen, liver, large and small intestines, and kidneys. The organs were chilled while the two-inch tumor was disengaged from the aorta, their main blood-supply, and from two other arteries. Then the organs were connected to new blood vessels and placed back in Brooke's body.

Brooke was thrilled to discover she had actually survived the operation and that virtually all of her organs had been removed and replaced. Her future is bright, her cancer is gone, and she is at home. She trusted the surgeon; but more than anything, she trusted God was ordering a miraculous operation!

Order my steps, dear Lord.

Thank you, God, for giving medical visions of healing to your physicians and for our willingness to trust them and believe in you. Amen.

When do you experience mountain-moving faith?

An Easy Life

My brothers and sisters, whenever you face trials of any kind, consider it nothing but joy, because you know that the testing of your faith produces endurance. James 1:2-3

Many of us wish for an easy life. We want to have plenty of money and resources that permit us to supply ourselves and our families with all we want and need. We never want to worry about paying bills or being able to take vacations or just doing whatever we desire. We want to be free of illness and suffering of any kind. We just want the easy life.

The easy life may be what we want, but it is probably not what we need. Problems strengthen our faith and produce endurance. Problems toughen us and help us survive adversity of all kinds. James writes that we should "let endurance have its full effect, so that [we] may be mature and complete, lacking in nothing" (James 1:4).

Consider the bristlecone pine trees. They live for thousands of years. We might think that they live so long because they live in good conditions, but that is not true. They live and grow where water is scarce and the wind is extremely forceful. They grow slowly so their wood is dense and better able to resist decomposition. Their root system is extensive and firmly anchors them to the earth.

Like these trees, if we live in difficult conditions, having to struggle for survival and resist winds of adversity, we will probably be better Christians. Our faith will be strong, and our prayer life will not only be consistent but continuous. We will probably learn to pray for strength to manage our difficulties rather than the removal of all difficulties. A wise person prayed, "Lord, don't move the mountain; just give me the strength to climb."

Order my steps, dear Lord.

Holy Father, help us face the difficulties in our lives and realize that the easy life does not prepare us to survive. Amen.

How has your faith been tested?

Long Prayers

O LORD, how long shall I cry for help,
and you will not listen? Habakkuk 1:2a

It seems some of us think we have to pray long prayers. We feel God has not heard us, and we need to pray a little longer. Some of us even think that the longer the prayer, the more likely it will be answered the way we want. I have even heard ministers pray so long that a sermon was not necessary. They had preached a sermon in the prayer.

I believe that God wants us to spend less time praying and more time doing what we are called to do as Christians. Instead of praying for God to feed the hungry, perhaps we should be out buying food and taking it to the shelter. Instead of praying for better children, we should be teaching Bible study or Sunday school. Instead of praying for those in the hospital, we should be visiting them.

God calls us to action. Habakkuk cried to the Lord for help. He wanted to know how long he would have to wait for God to do something. God told Habakkuk to do something. God told him to write the vision himself and to wait for it to be fulfilled (Habakkuk 2:2-3).

How many of us need to stop praying and get up off our knees and work? We need to do some of the things we ask God to do for us. God has equipped us with hands and legs we can use to do the work we want done. God has given us the brain we need to understand what he wants us to do. God has given us the resources we need to accomplish our tasks. We need to spend our prayer time thanking God for what he has already done. We need to stop asking God to do what we can do for ourselves and others.

What vision can you write today? Are you just going to keep praying and crying to God? God does not need your long prayers of supplication. He needs your praise and thanksgiving. He needs your work.

Order my steps, dear Lord.

Thank you, Father, for equipping me to serve. What do you need me to do today? Amen.

What prayers do you think God wants you to answer?

Unlikely Cures

Elisha sent a messenger to him, saying, "Go, wash in the Jordan seven times, and your flesh shall be restored and you shall be clean." 2 Kings 5:10

Have you ever been sick and in search of a cure, any cure? Did you seek out old wives' tales, desperate for anything? Did you discover some of those unlikely cures actually worked? I have.

When I read the story of Naaman, I wonder why he doubted doing what Elisha suggested. I know he thought he did not need to travel to Israel to wash in a river. There were rivers in Damascus, and surely their waters were every bit as powerful. Naaman refused to do what the prophet had suggested. (Read 1 Kings 5:1-19.)

There were several reasons Naaman refused to cooperate. First, he had asked his king for permission to seek a cure in Israel. Second, his king sent gifts seeking to pay for the cure, but those gifts were not accepted. Third, the king of Israel did not have the power to cure Naaman. Fourth, the prophet who did claim to be able to help Naaman did not even come out to see him. He just sent a messenger. Fifth, the instructions were too simple. What difference could washing in a river make?

Perhaps we are sometimes like Naaman. We doubt unlikely cures. I understand that in the late eighteenth century a milkmaid exposed herself to cowpox to prevent contracting smallpox. Most people thought her actions were ridiculous, but Edward Jenner paid attention to what the maid had done and eventually invented a vaccination for smallpox based on what she had done. We must be reminded that the word *vaccine* comes from the Latin word, *vacca*, for cow. Her unlikely cure led to a real cure.

Are we interested in trusting God for the unlikely cures needed in our lives? As we develop meaningful Bible study and periods of prayer, God will speak to us and prepare us for the unlikely cures he has already perfected.

Order my steps, dear Lord.

Father, thank you for the unlikely cures and the faithful servants who helped bring them into our lives. Amen.

What unusual or unorthodox cures have you been exposed to or been made aware of?

Forgiven and Forgotten

No longer shall they teach one another, or say to each other, "Know the LORD," for they shall all know me, from the least of them to the greatest, says the LORD; for I will forgive their iniquity, and remember their sin no more.
Jeremiah 31:34

Learning to forgive is very difficult, but learning to forget is even more difficult. That may seem contradictory because we are so good at forgetting. How many times have we forgotten a telephone number, an address, or a name? How often have we forgotten where we put our keys or filed that paper? How many times has that birthday or anniversary just slipped our minds? We are really good at forgetting things that do not hurt us.

I am so glad God is not like us. No matter how many times we sin against God or fail to worship him, he forgives us. God does not remember our sins or constantly remind us of them. We are quick to remind those we say we have forgiven of the things they did in the past. We may even tell them we forgave them once, but we will not do it again. If we are keeping records, are we really forgiving?

God spoke to Jeremiah of the new covenant he would make with the Israelites. God would put his law within them and write it on their hearts. They would be his people (Jeremiah 31:33). They would know him and know he was a forgiving and forgetting God.

Perhaps those that we are challenged to forgive ought to get to know us. They need to understand the laws by which we live; they need to appreciate our value system. If they really knew us, it would be harder to violate us and it would be easier for us to forgive.

When we really know and love each other, it is easier to forgive. It is not automatic, but it is possible. Just think of how many times God has forgiven us, and we can make an effort not only to forgive, but also to forget.

Order my steps, dear Lord.

Lord, thank you for being both loving and forgiving. Help me in my attempt to be like you. Amen.

In what ways do you forgive and forget?

Living Water

Let anyone who is thirsty come to me, and let the one who believes in me drink. As the scripture has said, "Out of the believer's heart shall flow rivers of living water."
John 7:37b-38

It is only when we are really thirsty that we realize we cannot live without water. We debate all the time about the number of glasses of water we should drink each day. Some of us even say that we do not like water and try to drink flavored water or substitute other liquids. Nutritionists have shown that we do get some water from foods and liquids; yet, there are times, even if we don't like water, when we just crave a drink. Nothing satisfies like water when one is really thirsty.

Have you ever noticed how plants just wither and die when they are water deprived? In 2008 there was such a drought in Georgia that water usage restrictions were placed on everyone. There were penalties for watering one's lawn or plants or even washing one's car. Showers were to be shortened, and flushing the toilet was to be minimized. Of course, many people did not bother to obey these last two restrictions, but lawns turned brown and flowers died. The neighborhoods did not look nearly as beautiful as they normally did. People even complained that they lost large amounts of money on the lawn treatments and flowers they had purchased.

I suppose the lawn and the flowers were thirsty. You could tell by the way the ground shrank and cracked that moisture was needed. Once the drought had ended, everything that had not died came back to life. The ground expanded, the lawns greened up, and the flowers bloomed. With some loving care, many lawns were restored to their original beauty.

If earth and plants need watering, surely people need water too. We need the living water Jesus spoke of. We need to respond to his invitation. We need to come to him as believers and drink of his wisdom. When we fail to spend time with him, we become parched and dry. We shrink and fade. We have no beauty and no nourishment for spiritual growth. We need his living water. We need the Word.

Order my steps, dear Lord.

Lord, I need your living water. I don't want to wither and die, shrink and fade. As I spend time with you, my roots are nourished and my heart overflows with your blessings. Amen.

What is living water?

One Day at a Time

Give us this day our daily bread. Matthew 6:11

One of the most difficult things one has to do is live one day at a time without worrying about tomorrow. My husband always says that tomorrow never comes. We have never seen a tomorrow. There is only today. Yesterday has gone and when tomorrow comes, it will be today.

Jesus told us to ask for bread for today only. He told the disciples to pray, "Give us this day our daily bread" (Matthew 6:11). They were to trust God to supply bread on a daily basis. They were not to ask for enough for months and years to come.

Why is it so hard to trust God to supply our needs day by day? In 2009 the United States economy was in bad shape, and there was an increase in suicides. Some people just didn't see how they would make it to the next day. They had lost faith, and they could not imagine living on less than they were used to having. Some of those who decided to end their lives also decided to end the lives of their family members. They did not want them to suffer or to have to live on less. They made faithless choices for themselves and their loved ones.

I wish we could all return to trusting in God and living one day at a time. God is able. God will give us so much more than we can imagine. Our responsibility is to know him, love him, and serve him. He will see us through economic depressions. He has done it so many times before. Only trust him.

Order my steps, dear Lord.

Lord, thank you for being a God who supplies more than we can wish for or imagine one day at a time. Amen.

What do you pray for one day at a time?

Finishing the Race

I have fought the good fight, I have finished the race, I have kept the faith. 2 Timothy 4:7

It's hard to forget the Olympic race in which a runner was hurt but did not want to stop running the race. The runner's father was there watching. Seeing his son struggling led the father to run onto the track and help his son to the finish line.

Then there was a young woman who had practiced for the fourteen-mile run at Pike's Peak. About a third of the way into the race, she knew that she could go no further, so she told her father, who was also running, that she was dropping out. Her father did not want her to quit, so he asked if she could keep going if he ran with her. She agreed to try, and although other runners passed them by, they finished the race together.

I know that those watching both of these children running with their fathers brought cheers and tears of joy.

There is something so moving about seeing fathers and children accomplishing tasks together. The father is willing to help, and the child is willing to try. What a blessing!

Do we rely on our heavenly Father for help in running the race of life? How many of us try to run alone or with others who know no more about the race than we do? Our Father has the knowledge, the insight, the experience, the love for us that no one else has. How could we even consider running the race without him?

So many of us think we have all the answers, and we are like a two-year-old who insists on doing it himself. We may feel that we are independent and all-sufficient, but we need God to lead and guide us.

I don't know about you, but I would not even consider running this race alone.

Order my steps, dear Lord.

Holy Father, thank you for being my running guide. I need your direction every step of the way. Amen.

In what situations have you fought a good fight, finished the race, and kept the faith?

Conflicting Reports

But Caleb quieted the people before Moses, and said, "Let us go up at once and occupy it, for we are well able to overcome it." Then the men who had gone up with him said, "We are not able to go up against this people, for they are stronger than we." Numbers 13:30-31

The Lord instructed Moses to send some men, a leader from each tribe, to spy out the land he was giving to the Israelites. The men went and reported back that the land was flowing with milk and honey and the fruit was sweet and delicious. However, they also believed the people were too plentiful and strong to be overtaken. They even said the people were so large that they felt like grasshoppers in their presence.

This was one report, but there was a conflicting report. Caleb told the Israelites they were well able to overcome the people who lived there. Caleb knew that God had said he was giving the land to the Israelites, and Caleb wondered what the size and number of the inhabitants had to do with God's promise.

How often do we doubt God's promises? God has promised to be with us, never to forsake us; yet we are afraid to move forward. Are we listening to conflicting reports? Are there those who keep telling us what we cannot do or cannot achieve? Have we forgotten or ignored God's promises?

No matter how great the obstacles or how difficult the task, God has given us the victory. The enemy may be a giant, and we may be grasshoppers, but God is able. Our job is to believe and not doubt.

Which report do you believe—the one that God has given or the one that the enemy keeps whispering in your ears? Whatever it is you are struggling with today, God says you can do it. Only believe.

Order my steps, dear Lord.

Lord, I believe. Help my unbelief. Amen.

What is it that causes you to believe one person's report and doubt another person's report?

Time to Die

Then [Elijah] went alone into the wilderness, traveling all day, and sat down under a broom bush and prayed that he might die. "I've had enough," he told the Lord. "Take away my life. I've got to die sometime, and it might as well be now." 1 Kings 19:4 TLB

When Elijah received word that Queen Jezebel was going to kill him, he fled for his life; but after traveling all day and feeling alone and lonely he asked to die. He had had enough, and he believed he would have to die someday, so why not let him die right then? If he really felt that way, why did he bother to run? He could have just let Jezebel kill him, for she had promised to do it before the end of the next day.

Like Elijah, we may think we want to die, but when it comes right down to it, we do all we can to live. We may learn a disease if left untreated may kill us. So we seek treatment. We may not have enough money to survive, so we seek assistance from the government or from charities. We want to live. We want to thrive. We don't believe it is time to die.

Now, there are some exceptions. One man who was suffering with cancer went to the hospital for treatment and observed the other cancer patients. He saw they had lost weight and hair. He decided that he did not want to be treated. He proclaimed, "I was a good-looking man, and I will die a good-looking corpse!" He knew that he would have to die someday with or without his hair.

Remember that Elijah thought he would have to die someday, but did he? There is no record of Elijah's death. He was taken to heaven by a whirlwind (2 Kings 2:1, 11). If Elijah had died when he asked to, there would have been so many missed blessings, and Elisha would not have been trained to succeed him.

There is a time to die, but it is not our call. We do not know what God has in store for us. There may be others we are yet to train, books to write, or seeds to plant. We may even be like Elijah and go to heaven in a whirlwind.

Order my steps, dear Lord.

Lord, help me live each day to the fullest. When it is time to die, you will take me to be with you. Amen.

Describe a time when you or someone you know thought it was time to die.

Strength from Weakness

But we have this treasure in clay jars, so that it may be made clear that this extraordinary power belongs to God and does not come from us. 2 Corinthians 4:7

If you consider the porous nature of clay and its fragility, one would wonder why treasure would be kept in clay jars. The treasure could easily be lost if the jars are broken. The treasure could also be damaged if the jars become damp or otherwise exposed to nature. Whenever treasures are kept in vulnerable places, there must be faith that protection will come from some other location. The jars are weak, but the protection that surrounds them is strong.

We are like those jars. Our bodies are weak, but God is strong, and we get our strength from him. How often have we heard someone say, "I just don't know how I made it up that hill! My body had given out. It must have been God." Or perhaps someone said, "I did not have the strength to go on, but God sustained me." When we are weak, God is strong. God is constantly ordering the steps of all those who believe.

Paul wanted the Corinthians to know that the extraordinary power that the Christians had did not come from within. God was the source of the power, and they were all engaged in ministry by God's mercy. No matter how they were afflicted, they survived. They were never crushed, broken, or driven to despair. They may have appeared fragile on the outside, but their strength came from within.

What can we learn from this? When we are afflicted, can we survive? We can if we depend on and draw from that extraordinary power that resides within. We know that God is in us and he is protecting us on every side. We are like the clay jars. We are fragile on the outside, but God provides the power that enables us to bear our burdens and live with the joy of being completely dependent on him.

Order my steps, dear Lord.

Thank you, Father, for the miraculous gift of your extraordinary power. Amen.

How do you recognize your weakness? Do you feel that you are strengthened by it?

A New Creation

So if anyone is in Christ, there is a new creation: everything old has passed away; see, everything has become new!
2 Corinthians 5:17

Have you ever wanted to get rid of all of your old clothes and replace them with new ones? Or have you ever wanted to replace all of your furniture? You may have felt new things would give you a new start and a brighter outlook on life. Because I have never replaced all my clothes or furniture, I am not sure what the outcome would be, but I have a feeling that nothing much would change. The same things that caused you to be dissatisfied with the old things would eventually cause you to be dissatisfied with the new things.

New things get to be old and ordinary. That is why we are always subject to changes in fashion. Our old things become outdated, and we want to be in style. The problem is that they are material things, and they cannot change with us. However they were made, they will remain.

On the other hand, people have the opportunity to change. We do not have to stay the way we were. We can change the way we look, dress, think, and respond. We can become new creations. If we are in Christ, we can become new creations. We cannot stay the same. We must adopt a whole new way of living once we begin to live for Christ.

Once one begins to live for Christ, there may have to be some wardrobe changes. Some of the old clothes just won't be appropriate anymore. Sin will have to be put away and replaced with service. Hate will have to be removed so that love can take its place. Joy will be seen through sorrow, and peace will reign over war. A new creation will emerge.

Order my steps, dear Lord.

Lord, help me change my clothes so that I can live for you.
Amen.

In what way would you like to become a new creation?

Starting Small

I fed you with milk, not solid food, for you were not ready for solid food. 1 Corinthians 3:2a

I have never really learned how to build a fire. I would try to get the fire in my fireplace started, but it would always go out. I used small pieces of kindling sticks and newspaper, along with my bigger logs, but the fire would go out, and my bigger logs would just smoke.

Eventually I discovered what I was doing wrong. I should have used only the kindling sticks and the paper to get a good small fire going, and then added the larger logs. I should have been starting small rather than trying to start big. Even though I think I finally learned the secret, when I built my new home, I had gas logs installed. All I have to do is flip the switch.

I think that many of us wish there was a short cut or a switch to flip that would make us well-seasoned Christians, but we have to build our faith with the small fires before we are ready for the big ones. We all are potentially very good and faithful Christians, and the trials and struggles we face make us stronger.

If we are fortunate enough to grow up in Christian homes, we see how kindling starts that small fire in our hearts. We go to Sunday school, youth meeting, vacation Bible school, and summer camp. We have the experience of learning, working, and sharing with others. We listen to and make our own testimonies of faith. We have an opportunity to give our lives to Christ. The milk we are being fed is strengthening our bodies and readying us for solid food. We are starting small and will grow in our faith.

If we become Christians later in life, we have the joy of surrounding ourselves with seasoned Christians. We need to join a Bible study, a new members' class, and a service ministry. The more we become involved in the outreach ministry of the church, the stronger we will grow in our faith. We need to learn to be servants, for that is the nature of our calling.

So start small, but keep growing in your faith. You must get the small fire burning brightly before you are ready to put the big logs on the blaze.

Order my steps, dear Lord.

Father, help me kindle my fire for you in such a way that it will burn brightly. Amen.

How do we know when church members are ready for solid food?

Failure to Forget

Then Peter came and said to him, "Lord, if another member of the church sins against me, how often should I forgive? As many as seven times?" Jesus said to him, "Not seven times, but, I tell you, seventy-seven times."
Matthew 18:21-22

Failure to forget may not be real forgiveness. When we fail to forget the act that required forgiveness, it stays alive in our hearts and minds. We continuously live with the act until we are irritated or hurt all over again.

Consider Linda who got into an argument with her sister. The argument ended when Linda's sister hit her with a stick leaving an open wound. Although her mother cleaned and bandaged the wound, Linda repeatedly opened the bandage and showed the wound to whoever would listen to her complaint. In so doing, she caused an infection to set in, and the infection was followed by an abscess. Because she refused to leave the wound alone, allowing it to heal, she suffered more damage. She could not forget what had happened.

Although it is hard to forgive and forget, real forgiveness involves forgetting. Failure to forget means we hold on to our hurts and disappointments, and they fester and infect our lives. We cannot live as Christians harboring resentment and holding grudges. We must strive to forgive over and over again—seventy-seven times. Then we must forget whatever it was that required forgiveness.

God has equipped us with forgiving hearts and minds. It takes a lot of effort, but it is possible. Let's give it a try. Just think about it: who do you need to forgive and what do you need to forget today?

Order my steps, dear Lord.

Lord, I want the true spirit of forgiveness to live in my heart. Help me. Amen.

What motivates you to forgive? Do you forget the past wrongs?

Sharing the Pain

Blessed are those who mourn, for they will be comforted.
Matthew 5:4

Jim was trying to recover from the death of his daughter. She had been hit by a car and had not survived. Jim and his wife and other children were devastated. They turned to each other for comfort, but found none. They were all suffering a great feeling of loss. They looked at each other and began to cry. How would they ever survive?

Then Jim was transferred to a new job. He thought being around people who had not known his daughter would help him recover. Once he became acquainted with his new coworkers, he discovered that several of them had experienced tragic family situations. Some of them had lost young children to accidents and disease. One coworker had a child with Down syndrome. Another had a child with cystic fibrosis, and it was uncertain how long that child would live. Then there were those whose adult family members were suffering with the final stages of cancer. One had a parent with severe dementia.

Each day the coworkers met for testimony and prayer. They talked about how they had learned to survive each day. They asked for prayer and support, and they prayed for each other. Jim even started to think death was not the worst fate his daughter could have suffered. He knew some of his coworkers were living each day with the slow and uncertain death of a child or family member. Rather than seeking to be comforted, Jim started to comfort others. Offering comfort and support to others helped him feel comforted. He learned to share the pain.

We are blessed when we mourn because we will be comforted. Perhaps our comfort comes from ourselves to others. Whom can you comfort today?

Order my steps, dear Lord.

Help us, Lord, to share your love and compassion with others. Amen.

How have you comforted one who was mourning?

Self-Examination

For there is no distinction, since all have sinned and fall short of the glory of God. Romans 3:22b-23

One of the most interesting things about us as human beings is our ability to see fault in others. We are quick to criticize others, but we rarely notice anything at all that may be wrong with us. I guess we just don't believe we have any faults. Even though we will agree that, "All have sinned and fall short of the glory of God," we still somehow feel that we are not included in that "all."

The news constantly reports that celebrities have cheated, stolen, committed adultery. Some of us may think celebrities are just too weak to resist temptation. We never even consider that our close friends and neighbors, and even we, have done the same things. We may even ignore or excuse these sins when ordinary people commit them; but, somehow we feel that celebrities ought to be able to resist these sins because they are so blessed with abundance.

Does having an abundance of material blessings equip one to resist sin? Perhaps the more one has the better one is equipped to sin. There is no worry about the cost of hotel rooms, airplane tickets, devoted fans to inflate their egos, and so forth.

But let us not be consumed with sins of the flesh. There are also sins of omission. We judge others who do not care for their parents or refuse to sacrifice for their children while we may be doing the same thing. We may excuse ourselves by saying our parents live in other cities and we have siblings who are physically or emotionally closer to them. We may claim our children need to learn the value of hard work or to do without the way we did. There are many reasons not to judge ourselves.

Take a long, hard look at yourself. What do you see? Do you see one who has sinned and fallen short of God's glory? Do you see one who is trying every day to be a better Christian? Do you see one who is making sacrifices for others? Do you see a real servant leader or one who seeks to be served? While you clearly see your neighbor's sins, have you missed your own? Examine yourself.

Order my steps, dear Lord.

Father, I know I have not been the best Christian I am capable of being, but help me resist finding fault in others while I strive for self-improvement. Amen.

What steps are you taking toward self-improvement?

A Language of Signs

Let anyone with ears listen! Matthew 11:15

Some people with ears listen, but they cannot hear any sounds. They listen to a language of signs. It is a beautiful language, and I often wish I had taken the time to study it. I have learned a few of the signs by watching sign language interpreters in church or other assemblies, but I have not become proficient.

When I watch sign language interpreters, I watch their facial expressions and their body movement, as well as the signs they make. Some of these interpreters are so good that one does not even have to know the signs to understand their meaning.

There was a man who brought his wife with him to church choir rehearsal each week. His wife was deaf, and he would see that she had copies of the music so she could follow the score and hopefully feel the beat. Whenever she seemed to have lost her place, she would look to him, and he would sign to her. The exchange between the two of them was beautiful, and everyone knew that they were communicating through the language of signs.

I have noticed the joyous faces of the members of congregations who are deaf when they are able to worship fully. They follow the lyrics of the songs and the message of the preached word. They even know when others are laughing or are tearful. They would miss so much if their interpreter was not present. Thankfully there are many interpreters in the church.

What language of signs do we present to others? I know there is body language that can show signs of welcome or dismissal. There are signs of love and signs of disgust. There are special signs that babies use when they want to be picked up or fed. There are nods of agreement and hand claps of joy.

The spiritual, "Certainly, Lord," asks, "Have you got good religion?" If one answers, "Certainly, Lord," then the spiritual admonishes that one should show some signs. There is a language of signs that shows one has good religion. Are we showing that language of signs?

Order my steps, dear Lord.

Lord, help me show the signs of Christianity through my language and my actions. Even those who are deaf should hear me loudly and clearly. Amen.

What besides your ears do you use to listen?

Woe to You

Woe to you, scribes and Pharisees, hypocrites! For you are like whitewashed tombs, which on the outside look beautiful, but inside they are full of the bones of the dead and of all kinds of filth. So you also on the outside look righteous to others, but inside you are full of hypocrisy and lawlessness.
Matthew 23:27-28

Some people appear to be righteous on the outside, but they are corrupt on the inside. They may live a visible good life, but they commit sin and destruction in places and at times that are secret.

Actions like these were very prevalent during Jesus' lifetime. He presented several woes to the scribes and Pharisees, calling them hypocrites. They appeared to be one way but were really quite different. I am always upset when I see people act as though they are friends with someone but talk about them and try to stab them in the back when they are not looking.

Consider the many Ponzi schemes that have been committed. Many people have lost their life savings because they trusted a hypocrite. They were fooled by one who pretended to have their best interests at heart. All the while the real reason for the pretended friendship was greed. They were lining their own pockets with the finances of others. Woe to them!

Let us try to live the same life inside and out. Let our words be honest and true. Let our religion be genuine. Let our church membership reflect our true discipleship of Christ. Consider the things that might cause Jesus to say, "Woe to you."

Order my steps, dear Lord.

Father, forgive us for all that we have hidden from others and have tried to hide from you. Clean us inside and out. Amen.

What steps do you take to stay clean both inside and out?

Be Still

The L*ORD will fight for you, and you have only to keep still.*
Exodus 14:14

The Israelites were afraid that they would die in the wilderness. They told Moses that they wished they had stayed to serve the Egyptians. They had gotten to the Red Sea and saw no way to cross. The only response Moses had was for them to stand firm and to have no fear. Moses knew God would deliver them, but he did not know how. God told him to lift his staff, stretch out his hand, and divide the sea so that the Israelites could cross over on dry ground.

How many times have we been afraid that we just could not go forward another day? How often have we wondered what we could do to change our situation? Perhaps we should have been standing firm and allowing God to fight our battles. Sometimes we must admit we are powerless and God is all-powerful. We need to stretch our hands to him and pray for a miracle. That's what Moses did, and the miracle was instantaneous.

What battle do you need God to fight for you? Are you afraid? If you are, you need to be aware that fear distorts your vision. You cannot see very well with fear in your eyes. You see monsters who are not there. How many times have you heard children claim that monsters are in their rooms because they are afraid of the dark? The monsters are really there. The children see them because their fear has distorted their vision.

Fear causes you to make bad choices. Because you are afraid that you will not have enough money to pay your mortgage, you decide to spend what you have on a good time or a last hurrah before you are put out in the street. Rather than sit still and wait for God's direction, you take it upon yourself to act in fear.

Your fear can also affect your prayers. You are so afraid you forget how to pray and to whom you are praying. Your God is all-powerful. Your God is not afraid, so why are you? Just as God delivered the Israelites, so will he deliver you. Put your fear behind you and just be still.

Order my steps, dear Lord.

Lord, there are times when I am so busy trying to solve my problems that I forget who you are. Help me take a deep breath and be comforted in the fact that with you nothing is impossible. Amen.

Describe a time when you forgot that the battle was not yours but the Lord's.

Timing Is Everything

He has made everything suitable for its time.
Ecclesiastes 3:11a

If you have ever played in a band or orchestra or sung with a choir, you know timing is everything. You must read your music and watch your director so you will know when to come in. Each instrument, each voice is meant to be heard at a specific time. When the timing is off, the music is discordant and hurtful to the ears.

It is the director's job to make each musician aware of the timing and to insist that each person watch him for his or her correct entrance. Practice sessions are imperative, especially if the musicians are not professionals. Once the musicians hear the beauty of the music when it is performed correctly, they want it to always be done that way.

I suppose that is why so many musicians are temperamental. So often they have had to stop and start the music over so that it could be performed correctly. They may even become impatient with the amateurs that participate. They know that the composer had a certain tempo and rhythm in mind, and the director wants to do it justice. When the choir or orchestra finally responds correctly, the result is beautiful music. But timing is everything.

God has also made everything suitable for its time. God knows its time, and we do not. We often want things to be done according to our time, but we are not in charge. God is. Just as the choir or orchestra director pleads with us to respond to the composer's wishes, we must also respond to God's direction. God knows when the time is suitable. We must learn to be patient. We must spend thoughtful time in meditation and prayer. We must worship with regularity and love and serve with abundance. In this way, we align ourselves with God's timing, for when we are aligned with him our lives are beautiful—just like beautiful music.

Order my steps, dear Lord.

Lord, I am your instrument. Help me learn your music.
Amen.

When was the last time you wished that either time would move forward quickly or stand still?

Mapquest

Jesus said to [Thomas], "I am the way, and the truth, and the life. No one comes to the Father except through me."
John 14:6

Whenever I am going to drive to a place I have not been before, I consult an online mapping service. I can put my starting and ending locations in the computer program and get a map or directions to the place I wish to go. It is interesting that I can get a fastest way or a shortest way, and I can also get the locations of nearby places of interest or intermediate stops. Somehow I always seem to choose the shortest way.

As I think about finding a way, I cannot help but hear Jesus' words, "I am the way." Some of us are looking for a way to live our lives. Eventually we may want to live a Christian life, but we make several stops along the way. There are points of interest we just must explore before we commit to the Christian way. Some of us even spend several years at these stops.

Think of the young adult who decided to stop going to church so that he would feel free to go to clubs and parties and live a life that he knew would be inconsistent with Christianity. He did not want to go to church with alcohol on his breath, so he just stopped going. He was not taking the shortest direction to the Christian life. He figured that he could always become a Christian later. He was killed in an automobile accident one night after a late party.

Then there was the mother who decided she was tired of staying at home taking care of her children while her husband was at work advancing his career. One day she simply left the children with a babysitter and never returned. She knew that it was not the Christian thing to do, but she was just so tired.

We may take detours on our way to salvation, but we all know that if we follow our map, our Bible, Jesus is not only the shortest way, he is the only way.

Order my steps, dear Lord.

Father, keep me on the narrow path to salvation. I don't need to stop at any places of interest. Amen.

What and/or whom do you consult for life directions?

Forgiving Love

If you love those who love you, what credit is that to you? For even sinners love those who love them. Luke 6:32

Sandra was a beautiful and vibrant young woman until she was hit by a drunk driver and left disfigured and paralyzed. Her mother, Monica, sat by her hospital bed and prayed for her daughter's recovery. She knew that Sandra would never be the same, but she prayed she would live.

While Monica was praying, Sandra appeared to be in a coma, but she could hear what her mother was praying. She also knew what her prognosis was, and she was not sure that she wanted to live. Sandra felt that life as she had known it was over. She wondered if she would ever walk again. She wanted to know what her face looked like. All she could feel was the pain and she knew that her face was covered in bandages. How would she face life in a wheelchair? Who would look at her with eyes of love and not eyes of pity?

Monica's prayer for her daughter turned into prayer for the drunk driver. Sandra could not believe how her mother was praying for the man who had destroyed her life. Sandra felt betrayed, but Monica kept praying for the driver. She prayed he would stop drinking and become an advocate for those seeking restrictions on driving under the influence. She could envision a young man whose life would be changed because he had carelessly gotten behind the wheel while intoxicated. She prayed that he would know he was loved and forgiven.

Monica's forgiving love was enough to bring Sandra out of her near comatose state. She had to say something to her mother. She had to ask how she could express loving forgiveness for one who had caused her so much pain. Monica did not hesitate to let Sandra know the accident had already occurred. Nothing could be gained by hating the driver. Perhaps some good could come if the driver repented. Monica told Sandra she needed as much love in her heart as she could muster because it would take all of her love and strength to overcome the paralysis and fight the pain. She told her that plastic surgery would fix her face, but that she would have to practice forgiving love to heal her heart.

What a wise mother Monica is. Do we practice forgiving love the way she does?

Order my steps, dear Lord.

Father, I know there are people whom I choose not to love, and that is not what you asked me to do. Help me love those who do not love me so that I may be a true disciple. Amen.

Have you ever prayed for someone who hurt you or someone you loved? Why or why not?

No Longer in Service

For I am convinced that neither death, nor life, nor angels, nor rulers, nor things present, nor things to come, nor powers, nor height, nor depth, nor anything else in all creation, will be able to separate us from the love of God in Christ Jesus our Lord. *Romans 8:38-39*

Geraldine's eighty-three-year-old mother died. She had lived a Christian life, been married for fifty years, and been a faithful member of her church. It seemed impossible that she was dead.

Geraldine was left with the tasks of seeing that her father was moved to an assisted living facility and that the phone and utilities were discontinued. She decided to call the old number just to make sure that the phone had been disconnected. When she called the number, she heard the recorded message, "The number you have reached is no longer in service." This message seemed to bring home the reality of the death of her mother. She was no longer in service as a wife and mother and church member.

Geraldine felt disconnected. Her mother was no longer in service. What would she do without her? Although she could not answer that question, she knew that she was not disconnected from God. God did not die. Nothing could separate her from him. She would never receive the message that God was no longer in service. God would always be available to order her steps.

What a comforting thought! Nothing can separate us from God. Death cannot separate us from him. That thought gave Geraldine hope. Her mother was dead, but she was not separated from God. Perhaps her mother was in service with God in heaven or perhaps she was sleeping, waiting for that resurrection day when she would be serving again. Either way, her mother was safe, and Geraldine knew that one day she would be in service again.

Order my steps, dear Lord.

Father, thank you for always being available. We are never disconnected from you. Amen.

In what ways have you ever felt disconnected from God? How did you get reconnected?

The Importance of Each Member

For just as the body is one and has many members, and all the members of the body, though many, are one body, so it is with Christ. 1 Corinthians 12:12

I read an interesting article about bees. Did you know that although a beehive may produce over one hundred pounds of honey in a year, an individual bee produces only a fraction of a teaspoon of honey during its lifetime? Just think how many bees it takes to produce a pound of honey. Although each beehive may have as many as ninety thousand bees, they all work together to produce the many pounds of honey. What if those bees spent their time fighting each other and being jealous of each other? They could not produce much honey.

Paul writes about the body and its many parts. He warns us that each part is important. Our body could not accomplish anything if it consisted only of hands or ears or eyes.

We need all of our body parts. We waste time wishing we had prettier hair or eyes or feet. We are blessed with what we have, and we must learn to use what we have to the glory of God.

Each member of the body, of the bee colony, and of the family is important. We need all of our body parts. It is interesting that when one of our needed body parts is weak, another part becomes stronger, compensating for the weak or missing one. I have heard many people who are blind say they can hear better than most people, and I have seen people who have lost a limb learn to do more with the remaining limb. Each body part is important.

We know how important each bee is to the colony. We cannot do much with less than a teaspoon of honey, but we can certainly make use of a pound. Consider the family. We know that there are many single-parent families, and we understand how difficult it is to try to do the job that was intended for two. Yes, each member is important.

And so it is with the body of Christ, the church. We need each member to do his or her part. All cannot preach or sing or teach, but each one can do something to further God's kingdom. Have you taken your spiritual gift inventory? Do you know what your special gift is? You have at least one or two gifts, and God needs you to use them in the church. Why not get started today?

Order my steps, dear Lord.

Father, thank you for each member of my body. Help me use them all to your glory. Amen.

How do you contribute as a member of the body of Christ?

Staying Onboard

Paul said to the centurion and the soldiers, "Unless these men stay in the ship, you cannot be saved." Acts 27:31

It seems that often when there is trouble or even suspected trouble many may decide to jump ship. This was certainly the case when Paul set sail for Rome. After sailing past Crete, the ship encountered a severe storm. The crew had to throw cargo overboard to keep the ship afloat. Paul tried to assure the crew that all would survive. When the sailors tried to escape from the ship on the pretext of putting out anchors, Paul warned they would not be saved if they did not stay onboard.

I wonder how many of us jump ship as soon as there is a hint of trouble. I know the divorce statistics bear me out. Just about half of all marriages end in divorce, and more and more couples fail to marry. They just live together until they decide the arrangement is not working. Many students drop out of school as soon as they discover hard work and study are required. And some parents abandon their children when they are difficult to discipline or when they ask for material things the family cannot provide. Yes, many of us jump ship.

Growing up in The Methodist Church where pastors are assigned for a year at a time, I experienced many changes in pastoral leadership. One year a new pastor was assigned. Before he even preached his first sermon, members were vowing to leave the church. They had not even given the new pastor a chance to demonstrate his leadership and pastoral skills, but he shocked them by telling them if they did not abide in the ship (the church), they would not be saved. Many of those members rethought their plans and remained.

I heard the story of a grandmother who drove a truck across bumpy and dangerous roads. Whenever she had the grandchildren in the truck with her, she would tell them to sit steady in the boat. She knew that she had the skill to deliver them safely to their destination, but she did not want them to try to jump out of the truck. She taught them to stay the course.

There are times in our lives when we just need to trust God to lead us through the storms. Life is not easy, but it is possible with God as our guide. Be faithful. Listen to his direction. Be constant in prayer. Stay onboard.

Order my steps, dear Lord.

Father, I know that there are times when we want to jump ship, but stay with us. Encourage us, lead us, and guide us. We want to be saved. Amen.

In what circumstances have you been tempted to jump ship?

Stubborn Soil

But as for what was sown on good soil, this is the one who hears the word and understands it, who indeed bears fruit and yields, in one case a hundredfold, in another sixty, and in another thirty. Matthew 13:23

When I first moved to Georgia from California, I noticed the ground was composed of red clay—not the black dirt I was accustomed to. My first thoughts were that nothing could possibly grow in that red clay. I wondered how people had gardens in their yards and actually grew vegetables and flowers.

I soon became accustomed to the red clay. I discovered sometimes people used potting soil or a clay mixture for certain plants. Other times, red clay was all that was used. Even though it did not look like fertile soil, it was.

Another thing about the clay made it difficult to use in planting. It became very hard. It was almost like rock, so it took a lot of effort to dig it up and create holes for plants. Again, I did not think it looked very fertile.

Then I thought about the way our hearts may appear to others. Are we hard-hearted, mean, and stubborn? If we are, we do not produce much fruit. Our soil is not good, and the word of God is choked and falls on deaf ears.

Dorothy tells the story of a disagreement she had with a friend. Her friend tried to apologize by offering Dorothy some flower seeds. Dorothy accepted the gift, but she did not forgive her friend. When Dorothy went outside to plant the seeds, she discovered the ground was very hard. She made no progress in the planting. She decided to wait until after it rained.

While Dorothy was waiting for God to send the rain, God sent her a message. Her heart was hard. She had no forgiveness within and she could not expect to plant anything that would grow. Dorothy heard and received God's message. She abandoned her stubbornness and opened her heart to forgiveness.

After the rain came, the soil was softened and Dorothy was able to plant the seeds. Dorothy had been able to forgive her friend. I wonder how many of us are surrounded by stubborn soil.

Order my steps, dear Lord.

Lord, help me soften the soil of my heart and forgive all who desire my forgiveness. I want to be open to the full fruit of your word. Amen.

Are the sermons that you hear sown on good soil? How can you tell?

Consider the Penny

Do not store up for yourselves treasures on earth, where moth and rust consume and where thieves break in and steal. Matthew 6:19

A study was done of the number of pennies that would have to be on the ground before anyone would pick them up. People walked over hundreds of pennies. They could not be bothered with stopping and stooping to retrieve them. After all, a penny is not worth very much. You cannot even buy a piece of candy or gum with a penny. Pennies take up too much room in your purse or pocket, and it certainly takes too long to count them out when paying for anything.

Well, I am from the old school and will stop and pick up one penny. I never pass a penny by. I feel it needs to be picked up and used. Once, when I was standing in the grocery store check-out line, a person in front of me was short one penny. I know she wished she had stopped to pick one up. Of course, I offered her the penny. I usually have one or two in my wallet.

I know that we don't value pennies, but should we not consider them as representatives of ourselves? We were not worth much, but God sent his Son to save us. God did not consider our value. He considered our potential worth. How much are we worth?

Jesus warned us against storing up treasures on earth, those treasures easily become corrupt and useless. So, we do not need to save pennies. We need to use them to help others. Our real value is in service to God, and we cannot serve him without serving others.

Jim found a penny in the church parking lot. He, too, was from the old school, so he stopped to pick it up. He noticed that it was scarred and bent, but he knew that it was still useful. He took it home, cleaned it up, and set it next to his Bible. Each time he looked at it, he was inspired to do something for someone. He remembered how scarred and bent he was, and he wanted to help someone else find salvation. He knew that the penny's worth was in inspiring him to be in God's service.

It only took a penny to inspire Jim. How much would it take to inspire you?

Order my steps, dear Lord.

Father, thank you for considering my worth as a person and for sending your Son to save me. Amen.

What treasures have you stored on earth?

Already Done

And she said, "Let your servant find favor in your sight." Then the woman went to her quarters, ate and drank with her husband, and her countenance was sad no longer.
1 Samuel 1:18

Hannah wanted a child. In fact, she really wanted a male child. She prayed so enthusiastically that her priest, Eli, thought she was drunk. I can imagine she was swaying and moving her whole body, putting herself into her prayer. But Hannah was not drunk, she was just calling on and pleading with God.

When Eli discovered that Hannah was not drunk but praying with great sincerity and enthusiasm, he joined her in prayer telling her to go in peace because God would grant her petition (1 Samuel 1:17). Hannah left Eli believing that her prayer was answered. It was already done. She went home, "ate and drank with her husband, and was no longer sad."

Do we join Hannah in praying with enthusiasm and then proceeding as though the prayer has already been answered or do we keep begging and pleading? When should we claim an answer to our prayers? When should we believe it is already done?

Perhaps the answer resides in our faith. Do we believe God answers prayer? Do we feel as though God will answer our prayers? Do we have the experience that lets us know God has answered prayers in the past and he has answered prayers for others? Have we made a deal with God? Have we promised anything in return for an answered prayer?

I suppose all of these questions direct us to our own feeling of self-worth. If we feel worthy of God's favor, we believe he will grant it. If we know we will keep our promises, then we know God will keep his. If we feel what we have requested is in accordance with God's will, we know God will grant his blessings.

I want to be like Hannah. I want to always pray with specificity. I want to pray with enthusiasm. I want to enlist the support of the saints. I want to proceed as though the request is already done. And I want to keep my promises with praise and thanksgiving. Then I will be assured that it is already done.

Order my steps, dear Lord.

Father, teach me how to pray and how to respond to your blessings. Prayer is not all about requests; it is also about praise and thanksgiving. Amen.

After you pray, do you confidently let go and let God; or do you hold on to your prayers, not sure that they have been heard or will be answered?

Needing a Boost

Therefore encourage one another and build up each other, as indeed you are doing. 1 Thessalonians 5:11

The story is told of a group of campers who went out bicycling. They started out in midafternoon and were sure they would return to their camp before dark. They selected a path that got very steep before it led back to the camp.

Some of the campers were good cyclists and had no trouble navigating the steep climb, but others felt as though they had tried to do too much. They stopped and tried to rest, but they found that their legs began to stiffen. They were not sure they would make it back to camp before dark.

One camper was about to quit when he felt a strong hand on his back. Another camper was giving him a boost. Just feeling that other hand and knowing someone was helping him reach his goal did wonders for him. He seemed to receive energy and stamina that had been absent just seconds before. Soon he was cycling easily and headed up the hill and then down toward the camp.

When he reached the camp, he talked with others who were telling the same story. Each of them had started to give up thinking they just could not make it when they suddenly got a boost. It just took a little boost to renew their stamina and recharge their energy supply.

As I read this story, I wondered why so many of us as Christians fail to notice others who are running out of steam in their walk with the Lord. Sometimes we see people who are depressed and discouraged. Some are even considering suicide, but we often continue on our way without giving that needed boost.

Look around today. See if there is someone who could use a boost. Perhaps it is just a word of encouragement or a phone call or a visit. God has equipped you to supply that boost. Do it.

Order my steps, dear Lord.

Lord, please help me be a boost-provider today. Amen.

How do you encourage others on a regular basis? Who do you encourage most often?

Standing in the Need

Pray in the Spirit at all times in every prayer and supplication. To that end keep alert and always persevere in supplication for all the saints. Ephesians 6:18

I occasionally attend a church near my home. They are a very small congregation, so at prayer time, they call out the names of those in need of prayer. Coming from a very large church, this was amazing to me. I could not imagine calling out the names of members of my old congregation in need of prayer. We would just list the names in the church bulletin and pray generally for everyone.

However, I know how important it is to be specific in prayer. We ought always to take the time to pray for each person by name. (I heard one man say to give his address, too, so God would know exactly who was being prayed for.) I really liked hearing the members of the small church call out the names of their family and friends. The pastor wrote down the names and then repeated them in her pastoral prayer.

Another church always gave the responsibility of reading the names of those who were sick or in need of prayer during the announcements. The reader on one Sunday had picked up the wrong bulletin and was reading the names of some who had requested prayer or had been sick some time in the past. It was amazing that even though those people had not requested prayer, they still needed it. One parishioner even wondered how the church knew he had a new aliment.

We all constantly stand in need of prayer. A spiritual says it well, "It's me, it's me, O Lord, standing in the need of prayer. Not my father, not my mother, but it's me, O Lord, standing in the need of prayer." We all need prayer, all the time. We may not even be aware of our own need, but we are in need.

Paul advises us to pray in the Spirit at all times and to keep alert and persevere for all the saints. We all stand in need. Pray for one another.

Order my steps, dear Lord.

Lord, it's me, standing in the need of prayer. Amen.

How does one pray in the Spirit?

No Mistakes

Do not be conformed to this world, but be transformed by the renewing of your minds, so that you may discern what is the will of God—what is good and acceptable and perfect.
Romans 12:2

I wonder how often, when judging by the world's standards, we feel we have made a mistake. I know I have made cakes that were so moist and light they fell apart when I tried to apply frosting. I thought the cake was ruined. It was a big mistake, but my husband and sons told me it had fallen apart in just the right places so they could get a bigger piece. They assured me the cake was not made to look pretty, but to be eaten.

I know there are many tricks that can be used to disguise cooking mistakes. One can cut a potato and place it in a pot in which there is too much salt, or one can take the crumbs of a cake and mix them with ice cream or JELL-O to form a new and delicious treat.

There are also sewing tricks that can be used to turn what would have been a dress into a skirt or a blouse with sleeves into one that is sleeveless. We can even add borders to pants or hemlines to cover up having cut them out too short. Yes, we can make some transformations, and often the new result is better than the original or intended one.

A little girl was painting a picture for her mother. She accidentally spilled some brown paint in the middle of the picture. The little girl was in tears, but her teacher assured her that there was no crisis. The picture could be saved. The teacher showed her how to turn the blob of paint into a leaf. Then she added a few strokes to make it look as though the leaf was falling. With a few streaks of red and green, the accidental blob was beautiful and added character to the painting.

How like all of those potential mistakes we are. What appears to be a disastrous turn in our lives can be transformed by God into a beautiful likeness of him. We don't have to be conformed to the world and its standards. We can be transformed into God's own likeness.

Order my steps, dear Lord.

Lord, let my mistakes be transformed by doing your will.
Amen.

What mistakes have you transformed into something positive and uplifting?

Never an Overload

Three times I appealed to the Lord about this [a thorn in my flesh], that it would leave me, but he said to me, "My grace is sufficient for you, for power is made perfect in weakness." 2 Corinthians 12:8-9

In Atlanta there are many backyard decks. It appears the decks were not built to hold too many people. I have heard of several that collapsed during a party or gathering. The decks were not built to handle an overload, and sometimes the people who were standing on them were hurt.

The carpenters who built the decks only planned for a certain amount of weight. I suppose that they never expected that weight to be exceeded. I am glad God does better planning. We might think we are handling an overload, but God knows how much we can bear.

Paul prayed three times that his thorn would be removed, but God knew he could handle it. God just assured him there was sufficient grace for him to survive. God even let Paul know power is made perfect in weakness.

Just when we accept our weakness, God's power kicks in and sustains us.

I wonder what thorn we have. I think some people find food is their thorn. They cannot resist eating much more than they need. They go to the extreme, gaining too much weight. In turn, the weight makes them weak.

But then one or two overweight persons will accept their weakness and decide that, with God's help, they are going to lose the weight. Some diet, some exercise, some work with a personal trainer; but all realize they need power to succeed. If they recognize that power as God-given, they do not collapse like the backyard deck. They stand up under their self-imposed weight and rely on God to help them change their ways.

There is never an overload when we rely on the power of God.

Order my steps, dear Lord.

Lord, you know how much we can bear. Help us accept our weaknesses and draw strength from your power. Amen.

What thorns in the flesh have you battled?

Imprisoned by Anger

No, in all these things we are more than conquerors through him who loved us. Romans 8:37

Have you ever gotten so angry you could not function? You might not have been able to think clearly or respond in a characteristic manner. If you have ever experienced this emotion, you may have felt imprisoned by anger. Anger has a way of separating you from yourself. You are no longer the person you want to be.

Many people have responded in anger. There are numerous crimes of passion. Husbands or wives kill each other or they may respond strongly to an issue that is big business to them because they are angry about little or nothing. Often the anger is brought on by liquor. Once intoxicated the husband or wife starts to batter his or her children or spouse.

We often hear of drunken husbands who beat their wives, and there are many women who beat their children. The children often feel imprisoned by anger. They have no way to escape the home. Wives may go to a shelter, but children have no idea of where to go.

It is interesting that there are several ways of looking at being imprisoned by anger. Anger can imprison us in such a way that we cannot function sanely, but anger also can imprison others who are victims of our anger.

I am so grateful anger cannot separate us from the love of God. Nothing can separate us from that. No matter how angry we get, God still loves us. When we are angry we need to draw on God's love to heal and sustain us. God's love can liberate us from our anger. God's love can inspire us to replace our anger with love. Love never imprisons us. Love frees us for service.

Whenever you feel anger taking hold of you, think about God's love. Pray for the courage to overcome the feelings that keep us from responding as Christians. Just remember nothing can separate you from the love of God in Christ Jesus our Lord. You are no longer imprisoned by anger, you are liberated in love.

Order my steps, dear Lord.

Lord, I feel your love all around me. Help me use it to be liberated from anger. Amen.

What things anger you the most? How do you overcome your anger?

Into God's Presence

When they could not bring him to Jesus because of the crowd, they removed the roof above him; and after having dug through it, they let down the mat on which the paralytic lay. Mark 2:4

Just how much trouble would you go to in order to bring someone into God's presence? Think about the four friends of the paralyzed man. They had compassion for their friend. They knew they could not heal him, but they had heard of someone who could. They did everything they could to get the man into the place where Jesus was. The crowds were too great. The house was too full, but they did not give up. They were the paralyzed man's friends.

Perhaps some of us, those who are so-called friends, would have given up. We could say that we tried, but there was just no way. Yet, the paralyzed man's real friends did not give up. They must have subscribed to the motto, "Find a way or make one." And they did. They made a way through the roof.

Have you ever wondered whose house it was and how that person felt when he saw his roof being torn away? Do you think the owner wanted to stop them? Do you think the owner asked who would repair the roof? There is no mention of what happened after the man was healed. The emphasis is on the four friends and the paralyzed man.

We must not think about the owner of the house. I am sure those friends who made a way to get their friend into God's presence had compassion on the owner of the house and helped to repair the roof. Perhaps some of the others in the crowd joined in and helped. There may have even been a construction worker or carpenter in the crowd. Remember that Jesus had some training along those lines himself. Perhaps he helped to repair the roof. I just feel God would not have allowed anyone to suffer as a result of a good deed.

The question still remains, what trouble would you go to in order to bring someone into God's presence? Jesus, God's Son, is still healing, and people are still sick and hurting. Who have you brought to Jesus? You don't even have to go through the roof; you can just enter through the door. Most of our churches have lots of room. Go get someone and take her or him into God's presence.

Order my steps, dear Lord.

Lord, you are waiting for us to go into the highways and hedges and bring others to you. Inspire us to be about that business. Amen.

When have you had to find a way or make one?

Installing a Gate

You shall love your neighbor as yourself. Matthew 22:39b

When Vivian's children were quite young, she and her family moved to a very nice neighborhood. They felt they had moved to an area that was more expensive than they could actually afford, but they believed God wanted them to live there. The schools were good, the shopping was accessible, and their church was close by.

Although the neighborhood seemed to be a safe one, Vivian noticed several of the homes were surrounded by fences. Vivian had always felt fences were built to keep neighbors away, so she told her children to stay in their own yard. She also felt a little self-conscious knowing her family did not have the financial resources the other families did.

The children were obedient. They played in their own yard, and they hardly ever played with the other children in the neighborhood. Vivian felt saddened by this because the children had lots of friends in their old community. All of the neighborhood children used to run in and out of her house, and she loved being mother to them all.

One day Vivian's next-door neighbor came to visit. Vivian did not know what she wanted, and she hoped that her children had not tried to play in her yard. But the neighbor greeted Vivian and told her how very glad she was to have a neighbor with children about the same age as hers. She then asked if it would be all right to install a gate between their properties so the children could have easy access to one another. Vivian was delighted.

Vivian stopped to think about the way she had misjudged her neighbor. Vivian was the one who was not loving her neighbor and seeking to be her friend. Someone once said good fences make good neighbors; but good gates make better ones.

What about you? Is there someone you have prejudged and not loved as a neighbor? Why not install a gate?

Order my steps, dear Lord.

Father, help me be a neighbor to all I encounter today. Amen.

Under what circumstances would you want a fence to separate you from your neighbor?

Something to Cling To

My soul clings to you;
your right hand upholds me. Psalm 63:8

Watching the fruits in my husband's garden grow has been a learning experience. One often wonders whether they are getting enough water and nourishment from the soil and whether they need support. Of course, the tomatoes needed a trellis, or they would fall on the ground. The watermelons and cantaloupes grow in vines already on the ground, so they don't need a trellis.

It is easy to realize we are like the tomatoes. We need support. We need something to hold on to in order to keep growing and developing in the right direction. Without our trellis, our faith, we soon topple over and die far too young. We will not have had sufficient time to reach our potential. We will not have developed into the strong, loving person God intended for us to be.

What trellis do you use? Is it prayer? If prayer supports you, are you praying as often as you need to? I started a practice of releasing balloons of prayer into the atmosphere. There were balloons of thanksgiving, balloons of praise, balloons of petition, and balloons of confession. Whenever I needed support, I would grab onto a balloon and pray the prayer I needed. Just knowing those prayers had already been lifted up gave me the strength and support I needed.

Is your trellis Bible study? I use that trellis too. I study my Bible every day. When I need its support, I think of one of the biblical characters who experienced some of the same things I am experiencing. I think of the way God guided and directed that character, and I hang on to my Bible trellis.

Is your trellis corporate worship? Sometimes we just need to be surrounded by that great cloud of witnesses who believe what we believe and confess their sins with us. Of course, I use that trellis and attend corporate worship regularly. Being with other believers gives me great support.

Just like the tomatoes, we need a trellis for support, maximum growth, and development. We all need something to cling to.

Order my steps, dear Lord.

Father, I am clinging to you. I know you will uphold me.
Thank you. Amen.

Describe a time when you needed a hand to uphold you.

Counting Blessings

Give thanks in all circumstances; for this is the will of God in Christ Jesus for you. 1 Thessalonians 5:18

Often I think about the many blessings in my life. When I am inclined to complain about something, I just stop and think of all my blessings. I have so many more things to be thankful for than I have to complain about.

I am reminded of the story of a missionary who was imprisoned under miserable conditions. For more than a year, he endured the worst conditions imaginable. Yet, when he was finally released, he had a story of blessings to tell. What kind of blessings could he recount after such a horrible imprisonment?

In an interview the missionary told how he survived the ordeal. He said he just counted his blessings every day. He thanked God for waking him up each morning. He thanked God that each day brought him a day closer to being released. He thanked God his family still loved him and was praying for his release. He thanked God for each day he experienced little or no pain. He thanked God for the simple pleasures of an occasional shower, a piece of soap, a few vegetables in his food, and water that was clean. How many of us have ever even thought to thank God for things like those?

How often we forget how blessed we are! We have shelter, clothing, food, companionship, family, and friends. We have so much. Are we counting our blessings? Even when we do not have as much as we would like, we still have so much more than so many others.

I recently spoke with a friend whose cancer had recurred. He said some people had asked him if he had complained to God. He answered he had not complained about the good things that had happened to him, so why should he complain about the bad things. We must learn to be thankful in all circumstances.

The apostle Paul learned to be content in all circumstances. He praised God in jail and in the temple. He and Silas sang hymns to God after they had been beaten and thrown in stocks. He knew the meaning of "Hallelujah, Anyhow," and he counted his blessings. How about you?

Order my steps, dear Lord.

Lord, I just want to thank you for my abundant blessings.
Amen.

Describe a time when you did not want to give thanks for the circumstances in which you found yourself. Did you believe it was God's will for you?

Freely Give

Some give freely, yet grow all the richer;
others withhold what is due, and only suffer want.
Proverbs 11:24

Have you ever noticed that stingy people never seem to have very much? Somehow holding on to what you have and never sharing with others leaves one unfulfilled. It is true that by holding on tight, one does not lose anything, but nothing else can be acquired. A tight fist is not open to receive.

Consider the farmer who sows seed by hand. He wears an open bag around his shoulder or waist. The bag is filled with seeds, and the farmer reaches into his bag and widely scatters a handful of seeds. Somehow the more seed he scatters or throws on the ground, the greater his harvest. The Bible confirms this in the verse, "The one who sows sparingly will also reap sparingly, and the one who sows bountifully will also reap bountifully" (2 Corinthians 9:6).

I am not sure how we communicate this message to others. We live in a society where everyone seeks to gather as much as they can for themselves. They scatter nothing. The feeling is often, "I got mine. You get yours." Are we afraid that someone might actually reap more than we do? Do we believe that one person can acquire all the wealth in the world, leaving nothing for the rest of us?

There is a Hindu philosophy that claims the path of desire is unfulfilling and contradictory. Worldly success can never be satisfied and is at best temporary. During economic downturns, many have come to believe this philosophy. It is said that Gandhi, who owned very little in life, told his wife that she only needed one sari (dress) because if she was wearing it, no one could steal it.

Let's learn to freely give of our time, talents, gifts, and love. The more we scatter, the more we increase.

Order my steps, dear Lord.

Father, help me sow bountifully in all areas of my life.
Amen.

Describe a time when you gave freely. What were the results?

Chasing the Wind

So I hated life, because what is done under the sun was grievous to me; for all is vanity and a chasing after wind.
Ecclesiastes 2:17

The writer of Ecclesiastes laments that one works and toils to accumulate possessions and then dies and leaves everything he has worked for to someone who does not appreciate it. He calls the hard work "vanity and a chasing after wind."

Have you ever considered chasing wind? How would you know if you caught it? The wind is not tangible, yet one can feel it. So, I suppose that as long as one can feel the wind, one has caught it. But what do you do with it once you have caught it? Perhaps the chase is vanity.

Then consider working for things. That is surely vanity also. We accumulate things to the point of being ridiculous. There is only so much we can use or wear or eat. We will die and leave everything to one who has not worked for it but will have the opportunity to use and enjoy it. Yet, the one who inherits does not appreciate the work that went into the acquisition.

The solution offered in Ecclesiastes is to learn to please God. Acquire knowledge and wisdom, for with these God gives joy. Joy is that commodity we desire. It differs from happiness, for we can be happy for a measurable period of time, but joy is timeless. We have joy in our hearts and souls. We may experience sorrow, but inner joy consumes it. When we are happy, joy extracts the essence from happiness and savors it for another day.

How do we find joy? We love God with all our heart and all our soul and all our mind. We study his Word. We practice loving each other, and we engage in acts of kindness. Self-indulgence is futile and amounts to chasing the wind. Wisdom and joy are given to the one who pleases God. Let's try to please him!

Order my steps, dear Lord.

Lord, I don't want to spend my life chasing the wind. Give me the knowledge I need to please you. Amen.

What is chasing the wind?

Hurdles

Endure trials for the sake of discipline. God is treating you as children; for what child is there whom a parent does not discipline? Hebrews 12:7

Have you ever watched a race and noticed a runner fall as he or she tried to jump over a hurdle? You probably made a sympathetic sound and then hoped the runner would get up unhurt and continue on in the race. We root for those who overcome obstacles or hurdles. We want others to succeed because we can imagine what we would want if we were in the same situation.

Have you ever wondered why there are so many hurdles to overcome? Is it really true that we learn discipline from our trials? And don't we all discipline our children in hopes they will become better persons?

I remember my mother having severe and painful arthritis in her hands. She would place her hands under hot running water and exercise them by opening and closing them. She never really complained, but I knew she was suffering. I had a secretary who also had arthritis. She said that constantly using her hands by typing helped to relieve the arthritis pain.

Now I have arthritis in my hands. I have tried hot water the way my mother did, and I am typing constantly on books and other things. I also exercise my hands and occasionally wear arthritis gloves and even take pain pills. It is a hurdle, but I do not let it stop me.

We all have some affliction or we will have as we grow older; however, affliction and hurdles are not limited to older people. Some young people are affected also. We discover it is to our advantage to eat the right foods and get enough exercise. It is a matter of discipline.

Most hurdles can be overcome through discipline. That discipline may include time for prayer and meditation. God has equipped us to survive, but we need to grow closer to him. We have not suffered to the point of painful death, but Jesus did. He suffered for us, and we have salvation because of him. Your hurdles are nothing. God will see you through.

Order my steps, dear Lord.

Lord, thank you for being there to pick me up when I stumble and fall. Amen.

What happens to children who are not disciplined?

In Need of Repair

All things came into being through him, and without him not one thing came into being. John 1:3

Whenever something breaks or is in need of repair, the first thing I do is look for the owner's manual. I believe whoever made the item is the best person to consult about its repair. Sometimes the manual is hard to understand or the specific problem is not addressed, so then it is time to call the manufacturer or a person trained in the repair of the item.

The story is told of a homeless man who was seeking shelter. He went to an apartment where he knew that many families lived. They were all poor and had stored their limited resources, considered junk by others, in the basement. When he was admitted to the apartment, the families told him that there was no room upstairs, but perhaps he could squeeze into a space in the basement. The homeless man did not care where he had to go; he just wanted to be inside.

After a while the residents heard beautiful music coming from the basement. They discovered that the homeless man had found a broken harp among the discarded junk. He had repaired it and was playing it. The owner of the harp asked how he had repaired it, and the homeless man admitted he had made the harp. He told them when one makes something, one knows how to repair it.

Just as we consult the manufacturers when something is in need of repair, we need to consult God when we are broken and malfunctioning. God made us, and he knows how to repair us. We must go to him with our illness in mind and body. He is able to restore us to good working condition.

Order my steps, dear Lord.

Lord, I often feel broken and in need of repair. Be my doctor and let me feel your presence so I might obtain the healing that only comes from the one who made me. Amen.

Describe a time when you wished you could contact the maker or creator of a broken object so that you could find out how to fix it.

Help When Needed

He gives power to the faint,
and strengthens the powerless. Isaiah 40:29

Some years ago my husband and I decided to sell our big house and move to a smaller one. We called it downsizing in light of the fact our sons were grown and gone. The problem with downsizing is you have to get rid of lots of possessions because there is no room for them in the smaller location.

I love to get rid of things. I believe we have too much stuff. We certainly have much more than we need. So, I gave away furniture, pictures, dishes, linens, clothes, books, and so much more. I found room in my new garage for my holiday decorations and other things I rarely use. I was delighted to see the smiles on the faces of some of the people I gave things to. I was especially touched by a young woman who did not have a bed or a living room set. She was so glad to get my extra bed and my living room furniture.

Although I did not need help to get rid of my things, I heard of an elderly man who did. Evicted from his more expensive apartment, he was able to find a smaller, cheaper place. He did not look forward to packing, and he had no help. He had to get ride of some things, but he did not know where to take them. He was not sure what he really needed or if he would be able to manage on so little.

Just as he was feeling completely overwhelmed, two young people came to his door. They had heard about his predicament, and they had come to help him pack. They also knew where to take the things he was discarding, and they sang hymns while they worked. The man's spirits were so uplifted that he no longer felt alone and powerless.

The young people were volunteers from a nearby church, and they often found themselves in the neighborhood looking for ways to be helpful. They had come in time of need, and the old man was grateful.

Who can you help today?

Order my steps, dear Lord.

Lord, show me those who need my help as I meet them today.
I want to be your representative in times of need. Amen.

How have you helped strengthen powerless people?

Picking Up the Pieces

I have become like a broken vessel. Psalm 31:12b

A neighbor's son tried to climb up on a cabinet to reach a jar of cookies his mother had obviously put out of reach. He was able to climb on a few of the lower shelves, but when he got higher, both the cabinet and the boy toppled over. There were broken pieces everywhere.

The boy felt broken also. He had been disobedient and had tried to get to the cookies he was not meant to have, and he had climbed up a cabinet that was not meant to be a ladder. He knew he was in big trouble, so he did the only thing he knew to do. He got up, ran to his mother, and begged for forgiveness. Of course, he had to help clean up the mess and promise never to try such a stunt again.

How like that boy we all are. We may try to get something we are not supposed to have and in the process we destroy things we need. Just think of the people who bet their entire paycheck on the lottery. They are trying to get the big jackpot, but they destroy the means they had of paying their mortgage and buying food for their families. Can they run to God and beg for forgiveness and promise never to do it again?

Sometimes we have to pick up our own pieces. We have to take stock of our lives and see where we are broken. What has caused our crash? How many broken pieces have we become? What will it take to make us whole again?

I am so glad that God never tires of our running to him. He lovingly picks us up and helps us put ourselves back together again. He always gives us one more chance. The thief on the cross knew he was broken. He asked Jesus to pick up his pieces, and even in that last hour he was made whole. Are you ready to turn your broken pieces over to God? Will you help him put you back together again?

Order my steps, dear Lord.

Father, all I can do is run to you for help as I try to pick up the pieces of my life. Amen.

Have you ever needed someone to help you pick up the pieces or have you ever helped someone pick up the pieces?

Identifying Signs

Either make the tree good, and its fruit good; or make the tree bad, and its fruit bad; for the tree is known by its fruit.
Matthew 12:33

A classroom teacher decided to take a cue from a judge. The judge had ordered that convicted drunk drivers attach to their vehicles a bumper sticker that said, "I have been convicted of drunk driving." Of course, no one wanted to do that, so all offenders tried their best not to appear before that judge. The teacher made signs students could wear depending on their behavior. The signs said things like, "I had to sit in the corner for talking in class" or "I did not do my homework" or "I had to go to the principal's office today." None of the students wanted to wear the signs, so the teacher told them they would not have to wear them if the behavior described did not truthfully represent who they were.

Is there something distasteful about wearing a sign that identifies who you are? Would we resent wearing a sign that identified us as Christians? What if that sign said, "I am a Christian but I never do good works" or "I am a Christian but I cheat and steal to get ahead" or "I am a Christian but I only love my family"? Would we want to wear a sign that told the truth about who we really are? Just like the teacher said, we do not have to wear these signs if they do not truthfully represent who we really are. Perhaps we need to change our behavior.

No one wants to be embarrassed, and wearing signs might be embarrassing. But what if our actions so clearly identified us that signs were not necessary? What if we could identify the Christian in the crowd because that is the one who stopped to help the elderly woman cross the street? What if it was easy to spot the Christian in the neighborhood because that is the one who volunteered to cut a neighbor's grass or take a neighbor a bowl of soup?

I participated in a game in which a blank card was pinned on my back. Participants were asked to write words on the card that described me. I could not see who was writing or what they were writing, but I was eager to read the card when the game was over. I was relived to discover words befitting a Christian had been written on my card. I would have been proud to wear my card, my sign, all day.

Think about it. What identifying signs would you be proud to wear? What word would be written on your back? Are you bearing good or bad fruit? We are known by our fruit.

Order my steps, dear Lord.

Lord, empower me to bear good fruit as I interact with others today. Amen.

How do others know you by your fruit?

Accessible Roads

In the wilderness prepare the way of the LORD,
make straight in the desert a highway for our God.
Isaiah 40:3b

When I lived in Chicago, the winter of 1967 was one to remember. Many roads were not accessible. Some people who were at work when the storm hit were not able to get home. Those at home were not able to get out.

I remember this so clearly because I was pregnant with my first child. The roads were not passable. Some of the pregnant women who went into labor during that storm were taken to the hospital in helicopters, landing on the hospital roof. I was in my seventh month, but I was sure I would be one of those who would have that treacherous ride. My baby was not born until April; and, although the roads were passable, there was still snow on the ground.

President Eisenhower is credited with commissioning a network of roads that became the nation's interstate system.

He was passionate about this because of his experiences during World War II navigating many twisting and dangerous roads. He knew national security was at stake. In addition to the Interstate Highway System, he saw that tunnels were constructed through mountains and bridges were built over valleys and bodies of water.

There is only one way out of my current Atlanta neighborhood. If trees fall and block the entrance/exit, we have to stay in. One night we were out during a storm, and we could not get home. We had to stay in a hotel until the road was cleared. It does not feel good to be blocked out of your own home, and I am sure there were several neighbors who wanted to get out but could not. Sometimes roads are just not accessible.

I wonder if Isaiah was warning us to always keep an accessible way for the Lord to get to us and for us to get to him. He told us to prepare the way and to make a highway in the desert. John the Baptist repeated this warning (Luke 3:2-5). Are we preparing the way for our Lord? Are we making a highway in the desert of our lives? Do we need to make a way for our Lord?

He has told us to love God and our neighbors as ourselves. He has told us to be just and merciful and kind, and to accept him as our Savior. He is always accessible, but we have to prepare the way.

Order my steps, dear Lord.

Lord, my desert has a highway especially for you. Come into my heart, Lord Jesus. Amen.

When have you encountered inaccessible roads? Where were you trying to go?

Frozen in Winter

Weeping may linger for the night,
but joy comes with the morning. Psalm 30:5

When my husband and I moved to Chicago from Atlanta after he graduated from seminary, we were told Chicago only has three seasons—July, August, and winter. Being from California I was not thrilled at the prospect of winter most of the year, but I soon learned the comment did have merit.

Our older son was born on April 22, and there was snow. Our younger son was born on October 1 two years later, and again I saw snow from my hospital room. Snow as late as April and as early as October almost eliminates Spring and Fall. It did appear we were frozen in winter.

I never adjusted to the winters during our six years in Chicago, and I remember how happy I was to move back to Atlanta and much warmer weather. I never complained about the heat because I was so glad not to be cold. I had been frozen in winter for the night, but the warmth of the summer, my joy, did come in the morning.

This experience reminds me of the times in our lives we believe we are frozen somewhere. We feel stuck and unable to move. We are in a rut, but we have to keep believing that our frozen place may linger "for the night," but thawing, moving, joy will come in the morning. The psalmist reminds us to sing praises to the Lord and to be faithful because God's anger is but for a moment while his favor is for a lifetime (Psalm 30:4-5).

Order my steps, dear Lord.

Holy Father, help us wait patiently for deliverance from the unproductive stages of our lives. We may cry for a while, but joy will come. Amen.

Describe the time in your life when you have felt frozen.

Holding On

Can a woman forget her nursing child,
or show no compassion for the child of her womb?
Even these may forget,
yet I will not forget you. Isaiah 49:15

Jenny was playing with her friends on her parents' farm. There were so many places to explore. There were barns to investigate, chicken coops to peep in, and wells with water to test. And please do not forget the many trees to climb. Some of those trees had beautiful apples or peaches that appeared to be ripe for the picking.

It was an apple tree that really got Jenny's attention. High up in the tree was a beautiful red apple, and Jenny decided to climb the tree and pick that apple. She knew that the limb on which the apple was growing was pretty high up, but she knew she could reach it. Jenny climbed up, but just as she reached for the apple, she fell and hit her head on a rock. The children screamed and cried because Jenny did not seem to be breathing.

Jenny's mother was outside hanging clothes on the line when she heard the screams. She knew something had happened to her child. She dropped everything and ran across the yard to the place where the children stood. Other parents had come running too. All thought that it was their child who had been hurt.

The sight was gruesome. Jenny seemed to be dead. There was blood on the rock she had fallen on, and some of the parents told Jenny's mother to leave. They would notify the authorities. But Jenny's mother did not listen to them. She went to her child, gathered her in her arms, and prayed. She could not leave her child, and she did not believe that God had left her. That mother held on for dear life, the life of her child, and her child responded.

Jenny had a cut and a big bump on her head, but she was alive. Her mother had found her fallen and hurt, but her love and embrace had revived her. God finds us fallen and hurt, but his wondrous love encompasses us, restores us to his service, and helps us hold on.

Order my steps, dear Lord.

Your divine love is our salvation. Thank you. Amen.

When have you or someone you know had to hold on? Did deliverance come?

Challenged to Forgive

Bear with one another and, if anyone has a complaint against another, forgive each other; just as the Lord has forgiven you, so you also must forgive. Colossians 3:13

A high school teacher was the victim of violence. One of her students attacked her, giving her a black eye, fracturing her shoulder, and bruising some ribs. She was hurt and frightened. Although the student was expelled from school, she found it difficult to return to her classroom. She said she kept seeing the student approaching her and attacking her all over again.

That teacher took a brief leave of absence, sought counseling, and allowed her body to heal. Then she retuned to the classroom. She learned that at the time of her attack the student had been on drugs and was completely out of control. He probably did not even remember attacking her.

The student entered a rehabilitation program and was allowed to return to school the next school year. He was not in the teacher's class, and she rarely saw him. She was not sure how she would react when she finally did see him.

One afternoon the teacher was in her classroom grading papers. She did not hear anyone enter her room, but when she looked up, she was looking right at the student who had attacked her. All of the old fears that she thought were gone returned. She did not know whether to scream or try to escape. The student saw she was frightened and tried to assure her that he meant her no harm. He just asked her to forgive him.

The teacher remembered the words of Jesus when he prayed his Father would forgive those who were crucifying him, for they did not know what they were doing. She knew this student had not known what he was doing at the time of the attack. The drugs were acting for him. As a Christian, she was challenged to forgive. She forgave him without reservation.

Somehow the act of forgiveness gave her the sense of peace that had escaped her. A burden was lifted. She replaced hurt and fear with love and forgiveness.

Order my steps, dear Lord.

Father, teach us to forgive the hurt and pain that others inflict on us. It is only when we forgive that we can experience love and peace. Amen.

Who have you had to forgive? How did you do it?

Unconditional Praise

Let everything that breathes praise the LORD!
Praise the LORD! Psalm 150:6

As praises go up, blessings come down" is a popular saying in church circles. I have never really liked the saying because it implies that we praise God in order to get blessings. It also implies that if we do not praise God, we will not be blessed. I don't believe God waits for us to praise him before he blesses us. That would imply our praise is conditional and so are our blessings.

A little girl forgot to say her prayers before going to bed, and the next morning she broke into tears. She could not be consoled, for she believed she had blown her chance to get what she wanted. If she did not pray to God and thank him, then he would not give her any more blessings. Her mother tried to assure her God is not like that. God understands when little girls forget to say their prayers, and he continues to bless them. His blessings are unconditional, and our praise should be unconditional.

I am sure many adults feel they have suffered hardships or have not been blessed because they have not praised God enough. God desires our praise, but he does not want us to praise him so we will be blessed. God wants us to praise him because we are so grateful for his love and the many blessings he has already bestowed on us. We ought to praise him even if he never does another thing for us. He has already done enough.

We, along with the little girl, need to learn to praise God unconditionally. We need to praise God because he is so good and he loves us so much. We need to praise God because praising him brings us pleasure. When we think of his goodness and all he has done for us, we ought to dance and sing with joy. We need to praise God because he gave his Son to die for us and to save us to eternal life. We need to praise God because he is worthy to be praised. Hallelujah!

Order my steps, dear Lord.

Father, I thank you and praise you for your great goodness to me. Thank you. Amen.

What pattern of praise do you follow?

Porch or Patio?

Welcome one another, therefore, just as Christ has welcomed you, for the glory of God. Romans 15:7

When I first moved to Atlanta, Georgia, from Berkeley, California, I was surprised to see people sitting outside on their front porches. They would wave to passersby and even invite them inside for a cool drink in the hot Georgia sun. I decided that they were demonstrating southern hospitality.

Then when my husband and I moved to Chicago, Illinois, we decided to sit on the front porch and wave and greet passersby. They looked at us as though we were crazy. There was definitely no southern hospitality there. We finally took our chairs inside and kept to ourselves.

I have noticed since our return to Atlanta that instead of front porches, people now have backyard patios. They have their guests come to the back and be greeted and welcomed in private. You have to have an invitation to the patio.

Do we greet people and let our Christianity show in public—on the front porch—or do we hide our Christianity in the back on the patio? Is our religion practiced in private or is it practiced where all can see it? What are the signs of welcome? Do we greet each other with hugs or do we say a quiet hello?

Paul let the Romans know the gospel was for everyone and we should share it boldly. We need a front porch religion. We need to wave and smile and offer refreshments as we demonstrate the glory of God. Will people think we are crazy? Will we have to take our chairs inside the way my husband and I did in Chicago, or will we dare to do what Paul advised and witness boldly? Porch or patio?

Order my steps, dear Lord.

Lord, I want to be a bold witness for you. Amen.

What is a front-porch religion, and what is a backyard patio religion? Which do you practice?

Internet Junkies

For where your treasure is, there will your heart be also.
Matthew 6:21

I know several people who cannot start their day without logging on to the Internet. They have to see what is going on in the world; check their Facebook page, Twitter account, e-mails; and start to read jokes and tips from their e-mail buddies. They are Internet junkies. They need their morning fix.

Most hotels have caught on to the phenomenon, so they offer free Internet connections and even computers for use by their guests. There was a day when you had to pay to get an Internet connection, or you had to bring your own computer; but no more. Now junkies can get their morning fix on the road.

One young woman told me the only way she communicates with her family is through the Internet. As soon as her coffee is ready in the morning, she logs on. She can update all of her family members at the same time by sending an e-mail to everyone. Then she waits for responses from each family member. She says although it is so much fun, it takes up much of her morning. Once she has had her fix, she hurriedly moves to the other tasks of the day.

One morning she read an e-mail about spending time with God. She realized she had stopped her morning meditations when she purchased her computer. She rarely read her Bible or any of the devotional books she once read daily. Although she felt her connection to her family was stronger, she knew her connection to God was weaker.

What earthly treasure are we putting before God? Jesus reminded us not to store up treasures on earth. Those treasures will not last, but treasures stored with God will last forever. Is your Internet connection more important than your God connection?

Order my steps, dear Lord.

Father, thank you for the brilliant people who invented the Internet, but don't let me put it before you. Amen.

How much time do you spend on the cell phone or computer, and how much time do you spend with God?

Symbols of Belonging

Do not be conformed to this world, but be transformed by the renewing of your minds, so that you may discern what is the will of God—what is good and acceptable and perfect.
Romans 12:2

There is something unique about being in the world but not of the world. We are charged as Christians not to be conformed to this world. Although we live in the world, we do not have to take on worldly characteristics. When people see us, they ought to recognize some symbols of our belonging to that unique group of believers who profess Christianity.

It is interesting to note the various symbols of belonging. I notice people wearing crosses and placing the Christian symbol of the fish on their cars. I take note of people who have license plates bearing the symbols of the college or university they attended. I see the Greek letters on their clothing symbolizing the fraternal organization with which they are affiliated.

My particular sorority makes it clear that whenever we are in nightclubs or drinking (in the world), we are not to have on our sorority letters or symbols. Such conduct is not becoming to a member of an organization based on Christian principles. Also, we are not to wear pants, sexy sandals, or any inappropriate attire to ritual ceremonies or business meetings. Yet, I have not heard the church make any such demands.

Perhaps church membership has declined because the church has become too worldly. The church has conformed to the world. There is no longer a difference between church attire and everyday attire. We can no longer distinguish between a Christian driver and one who does not bear a fish on her or his car. That so-called Christian driver is just as likely to cut in front of you or fail to courteously let you in as one who bears no symbols of faith.

Our symbols of belonging ought to mean something. Our conduct ought to reflect our membership. We ought not be conformed to this world, but transformed by the renewing of our minds. Then we will be able to discern the will of God and will know what is "good and acceptable and perfect."

Order my steps, dear Lord.

Lord, I want others to know that I belong to you. Amen.

How do you discern the will of God? Do you believe that you conform to the world?

Why Not Adopt?

See what love the Father has given us, that we should be called children of God; and that is what we are.
1 John 3:1a

I have often wondered why so many single women opt to have biological children rather than adopt children. They seem to think somehow they will love biological children more than they would love adopted children.

I do understand the need or desire some women have to physically give birth. Many of us want that experience, especially if we had loving mothers. We want to be able to give and receive that same kind of unconditional love.

The problem is we do not consider the difficulties of carrying and bearing a child alone. There are those moments of the first time the baby kicks and there is no one to share that with. Then there is the reality there is no one to experience the birth and delivery with. There is no one else who can say with pride and joy, "This is my child!" But perhaps, most important of all to me is the family unit established by God has been broken. Although the birth may have occurred through artificial insemination or egg implantation, somehow that which is sacred to marriage has been violated.

Of course, you may not agree with me, and that is fine. However, I think of all the already existing children in need of loving homes, and I wish that some of these single mothers had chosen to adopt one of them. I think they would have discovered once a child becomes a part of your family, love grows. I even remember hearing a mother of both adopted and biological children claim the adopted ones were much more loving than the biological ones.

If we think about our membership in the family of God, we are all adopted. We are God's children because he loves us, and according to Romans 8:14 we are God's children if we are led by the Spirit of God. We are adopted. Think about it.

Order my steps, dear Lord.

Father, thank you for adopting us. We are your children. Amen.

If you were a single woman, would you opt for biological or adopted children? Would you be able to love each equally?

Learning to Dream

Encourage one another and build up each other.
1 Thessalonians 5:11

How soon do we learn to dream? Do you think toddlers have dreams, and do they share them? When my granddaughter was three years old, she dreamed of renting a bus and taking her friends to Washington, DC, to see the president. A six-year-old boy told his friend he was going to high school someday if he ever got out of the first grade. What dream do you have?

When I was writing my first book, I was told to tell others about it. The feeling was if you kept saying it, you would be encouraging yourself to continue with your project. I suppose we don't want others to keep asking us when we were ever going to finish that book we had been talking about. I know I took pride in telling people not only had I finished the first book, but I had written several more.

I wonder whether learning to dream involves learning to share that dream. As soon as we are able to formulate a dream, sharing it gives it reality. If we never share it, no one knows it exists. We need confirmation from others. We need to know they have heard us and they join with us as we pursue our dreams. Of course, we can be negatively impacted by the opinions of others. If they do not support us in our pursuit, we may stop dreaming.

I look to the Scriptures as I turn my thoughts to dreaming. "Encourage one another and build up each other" (1 Thessalonians 5:11). If persons trust us enough to share their dreams, no matter how young or old they are, let us support them. We ought to be grateful that they consider us to be a person who believes in dreams. We just may have the opportunity to encourage the next president of the United States or the next anointed preacher of God.

Order my steps, dear Lord.

Father, thank you for our dreams. Help us encourage ourselves and others as we envision our dreams becoming reality. Amen.

Whose dreams have you listened to? How have you encouraged them?

Trust God!

Jesus answered them, "Have faith in God." Mark 11:22

The dying words of a beloved minister were, "Trust God!" There is a woman who did just that. Her name is Mary, and she decided to go back to school and earn a degree. As a single mother of three children, every penny she had went to the care of her family. But she decided to trust God. She took her lunch to school every day and really scrounged around to find money for bus tokens and something to drink with her lunch.

One Friday afternoon Mary realized that she had only one token left and no money. She knew when she used that token she would have no way of getting back home. Shortly after making this discovery, she got a call from a doctor she occasionally worked for. He wanted her to work the next day. Mary felt relieved. She would go to work, and the doctor would pay her. She just hoped she would get off in time to go to the bank to cash her paycheck.

Mary used her last token to get to work, and she worked all day. In fact, she worked so late she knew all the banks were closed, and, more importantly, the doctor had not even mentioned paying her for that day. She did not panic. She just remembered to trust God.

As Mary called out to the doctor that she was leaving, he told her to wait. Then he said he had forgotten his checkbook and would pay her in cash. She had trusted God, and he had not failed.

Wouldn't it be wonderful if we all learned to trust God! I wonder what our faith would reveal.

Order my steps, dear Lord.

God, thank you for another day in which to learn to trust You. Amen.

Can you testify to a time you trusted God?

In Step with God's Word

All our steps are ordered by the LORD;
how then can we understand our own ways?
Proverbs 20:24

I believe when we consciously seek to follow God's word, our lives will be blessed. We will still have trials, for we grow as we face and triumph over difficulty. Our lives would be boring if everything always worked perfectly, but we don't have to worry because that is not God's plan for us. God has ordered our steps. All we have to do is follow them in faith.

Marsha did not know how she would pay her rent. Her boyfriend had left her with no food and no car. She could not believe he had eaten all the food in the house and had then driven off with her car. She was stranded, and she thought he loved her. What was she going to do?

Some of her girlfriends had already told her that her man was no good. All he wanted was her body, her food, and her car. What kind of love was that? It was time to regroup and focus on paying the rent. At least she still had her job, and she could get a ride to work.

While she was getting ready for work, one of her fellow church members called and asked if she had her tithe. The church really needed the money for some outreach commitments. Marsha had been faithful in paying her tithe, but this new situation meant that she could not pay her tithe and her rent. Did she have enough faith to believe God would provide her with rent money if she paid her tithe?

Marsha reflected on her conduct with her boyfriend. Had she been in step with God? Had she been following the steps God had ordered or had she been doing her own thing? Was God giving her an opportunity to get back in step with him by trusting him to provide for all her needs? Was God calling on her to put him first?

While Marsha was deciding what to do, she remembered the Scripture she had learned about tithing. "Bring the full tithe into the storehouse, so that there may be food in my house, and thus put me to the test, says the LORD of hosts; see if I will not open the windows of heaven for you and pour down for you an overflowing blessing" (Malachi 3:10). Marsha realized that she had never seen the righteous forsaken or their seed begging for bread. She knew being in step with God meant paying her tithe.

Order my steps, dear Lord.

Holy Father, give me the faith that will keep me in step with you. Amen.

In what ways are you in step with God?